Getting By or Getting Better

Applying Effective Schools
Research to Today's Issues

Wayne Hulley

Linda Dier

Solution Tree | Press
a division of
Solution Tree

555 North Morton Street
Bloomington, IN 47404
800.733.6786 (toll free) / 812.336.7700
FAX: 812.336.7790

email: info@solution-tree.com
solution-tree.com

Printed in the United States of America

12 11 10 09   2 3 4 5

FSC

Mixed Sources

Product group from well-managed
forests and other controlled sources

Cert no. SW-COC-002283
www.fsc.org
© 1996 Forest Stewardship Council

ISBN 978-1-934009-40-6

This book is dedicated to the educators who have enriched our writing by sharing their stories and strategies. Their passion, commitment, and leadership are embodied in these words from Kathryn E. Nelson:

Leadership is not a goal. It's a way of reaching a goal. I lead best when I help others to go where we've decided to go. I lead best when I help others to use themselves creatively. . . . To lead is to serve . . . to give . . . to achieve together.

Table of Contents

About the Authors

Wayne Hulley is president of Canadian Effective Schools, Inc., in Burlington, Ontario, an organization that provides educators with research-based tools and training to support school improvement efforts. In partnership with Lawrence Lezotte, Wayne addresses the needs of practitioners as they face the challenges of school reform. Wayne engages audiences with his humor, knowledge, and positive perspective. He has presented hundreds of programs on personal and organizational effectiveness throughout North America. In addition, Wayne created a site-based planning model that is used in more than 1,200 schools throughout Canada and the United States. His expertise encompasses assessment, effective schools research, and best practices for school improvement.

Linda Dier is a senior consultant with Canadian Effective Schools, Inc. She administers the Canadian Effective Schools League, an online research index that supports busy educators by providing immediate access to current research on today's educational issues. Linda is also a partner in LDG Consulting Group and works with teachers and administrators to facilitate planning along with ongoing professional growth and learning. Her expertise encompasses team-building, effective schools research, best practices in planning for school and student success, and assessment. Linda lives in British Columbia on Vancouver Island.

Preface

We can live our lives getting by, or we can commit to getting better. Getting by does not mean that we don't work hard and try to do our best. It means that we are not achieving the results that we desire or are capable of achieving. Getting better is about making a difference. Getting better requires resolve, planning, and action. Our observation is that schools that are getting better are doing similar things. While it is true that each school has a unique culture, we believe that all must address common issues to improve. When schools plan to improve, they actively work to shift their school's culture to become more effective in all areas. Getting better is not easy. The power of the existing culture can be formidable, and the temptation to take the path of least resistance can be strong.

In *Harbors of Hope* (Hulley & Dier, 2005), we presented the Planning for School and Student Success model, a process that supports school improvement efforts. In this book, we focus on the results that can be achieved when a solid planning process is used consistently. Our intention is to provide viable school improvement strategies that are supported by a solid research base. A wide range of practical approaches are illustrated through lessons learned in real schools that can prove they are not just getting by. They are, in fact, getting better.

We chose effective schools as the primary research base for our work because it provides school improvement teams with a comprehensive framework for identifying, categorizing, and solving the problems that schools and school districts face. The effective schools correlates are based on over 30 years of documented successes of effective schools. The correlates offer hope and inspiration to those struggling to improve. In our observations, we continue to affirm that the seven correlates of effective schools have withstood the test of time and marvel at the fact that they are versatile enough to be as applicable in today's world as they were when they were first identified.

The correlates as they were initially understood are now referred to as first-generation correlates. Over the years, a second generation of correlates has emerged in response to the ever-changing and diverse demands being placed on schools. The first generation correlates form the foundation. They are the prerequisite correlates that, if not in place, will make the emergence of the second generation impossible. No other body of research or school improvement process can make this claim.

Since *Harbors of Hope* was published, we have watched and worked with many schools across North America. When we reflected on the issues that are common to all improving schools, we identified seven common themes and began to refer to them as "lessons from successful schools." Embedded in all of the lessons are the correlates. What we have observed in schools that are making a difference is that they provide wonderful examples of second-generation correlates in action.

One of the great delights in writing this book has been the opportunity to meet and learn from the gifted educators who have shared their stories with us. We started our field-based research with submissions detailing successes from 45 schools representing 21 school boards in seven Canadian provinces. All their submissions contained rich information; we were impressed by the creativity and quality of work reflected in them. Unfortunately, the sheer volume of information presented to us by the original 45 schools made it impossible to include all their stories. We were forced to make some difficult choices. Appendix B includes the names of all schools that responded to our initial request for participation. An asterisk (★) denotes those schools whose stories are told here.

Chapter 2 details the process used to carry out the research for this book. Unless otherwise noted, the information used was provided by the principals of the schools involved, usually in consultation with staff. Initially it was gathered in the form of responses to specific questions we asked; however, as the research progressed, the principals involved also generously provided additional documentation to help tell their story. Such documentation included things like school-based planning materials, samples of personal writing, and graphs or tables showing school-based data and provincial test results. Personal contact via telephone and email was used extensively to confirm and clarify details. In all cases, the principals involved participated in finalizing their school's story and gave permission for it to be included in the final manuscript. The data in this book, unless otherwise referenced, are drawn from these direct, unpublished sources.

Deciding how to feature each school's story posed some interesting challenges, because they all reflect the seven lessons we have identified, and all of them are powerful examples of second generation correlates at work in today's educational context. After some deliberation, we chose to attach each school to one of the lessons and then highlight specific aspects of its story to illustrate the lesson and correlate being featured in it. The fact of the matter is that all the schools illustrate all the lessons effectively. That is why we call them "Harbors of Hope."

In 1982, Ron Edmonds, who began the effective schools movement with Wilbur Brookover and Larry Lezotte, stated:

> We can, whenever and wherever we choose, successfully teach all children whose schooling is of interest to us. We already know more than we need to do that. Whether or not we do it must finally depend on how we feel about the fact that we haven't so far. (p. 11)

It is our hope that you find *Getting By or Getting Better* both informative and practical. It has been our pleasure to celebrate and share the wonderful work being done by our colleagues. We believe that all schools have the option of getting by or getting better. We hope this book will help you make the right choice.

—Wayne and Linda

Section I

Our Learning Journey

1

Where We Have Been

In *Harbors of Hope: The Planning for School and Student Success Process* (Hulley & Dier, 2005), we shared what we believe to be true about schools that make a difference for all students. We called these schools "Harbors of Hope." Our thinking for the book was framed within a lexicon of hope. In our view, hope is a form of optimism that may seem unwarranted in the face of incredible odds. It is the thing that keeps people keeping on instead of giving up. Hope is not a naïve view of the world that is characterized by a blind belief that somehow everything will turn out all right. Rather, it is a realistic acknowledgement of existing challenges coupled with profound commitment to finding the means and resources to deal with them. It is a powerful emotion that fuels all activity in schools that are Harbors of Hope. We believe that schools become Harbors of Hope when staffs commit themselves to identifying and addressing anything that interferes with school and student success.

Effective schools research, which has been conducted for over 30 years, provided the foundation for our work in *Harbors of Hope*. Its power resides in the fact that the seven correlates of effective schools that were identified so long ago set the standard for effective schools and have withstood the test of time. While the educational context has changed dramatically over 3 decades, the correlates remain as relevant as ever. What has changed, however, is how they are manifested in schools. A second generation of the correlates has evolved over the years in response to the changing climate and demands in education. Student achievement, attendance, attitude, and behavior remain the key indicators of school effectiveness, and collaboration is the vehicle for change.

Our observation is that schools that are Harbors of Hope exhibit all of the correlates within a framework of *character* and *competence*. They demonstrate moral and ethical excellence (character) along with the knowledge and capacity (competence) to help all students learn. Figure 1-1 (page 4) illustrates the correlates within the character/competence framework. It also shows the key indicators of school effectiveness.

Seven Correlates of Effective Schools

1. Clear and focused mission

2. Safe and orderly environment

3. Positive home/school relations

4. Climate of high expectations for success

5. Frequent monitoring of student progress

6. Opportunity to learn and time on task

7. Instructional leadership

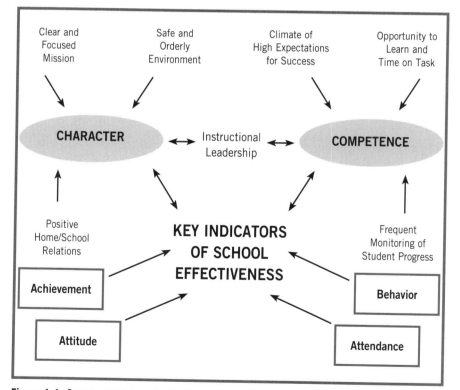

Figure 1-1: Seven correlates of effective schools linked to character, competence, and the key indicators of school effectiveness

Key Indicators of School Effectiveness

An effective school is one in which, over time, students show improved achievement, more positive attitudes, better attendance, and more appropriate behaviors. Teachers are often inclined to think that of the four indicators, attitude is the one that has the greatest impact on school effectiveness. Effective schools research has found, however, that schools and teachers cannot change attitudes directly. What teachers *can* directly influence is achievement through accurate assessment and effective instructional practice. As achievement improves, students become more positive about school, and, interestingly, teachers tend to become more positive about the work they are doing as teachers.

The Shift From First to Second Generation Correlates

Since the effective schools correlates were identified, expectations for schools and students have changed significantly. The body of research about best practices in teaching and learning has grown dramatically, and schools are being asked to respond to a wide range of student needs, community expectations, and government mandates. New insights about assessment, special learning needs, brain development, curriculum design, staff collaboration, accountability, and staff development have had a major impact on the work being done in schools. These insights, coupled with new external demands being placed on schools, have resulted in the evolution of a second generation of correlates that represent a developmental stage beyond the first generation. The first generation correlates provide a foundation that must be in place for schools to improve. The second generation, when successfully implemented, will move schools even closer to the mission of "learning for all."

Character Correlates

The character correlates are those that influence the moral and ethical aspects of our work with students. They focus on the relationships, values, and ideals that ultimately shape a school's character.

Clear and Focused Mission

In the first generation of this correlate, the focus was on teaching the students. The emphasis was on teachers taking responsibility for delivering programs that ensured all students achieved the school's curricular goals. The "learning for all" mission was about teaching students.

The second generation emerged as a result of the changing needs of students and altered expectations for schools. Integration of special education students, increasing populations of minority students, concern for the success of students living in poverty, accountability demands, and the expansion of curricula to include such things as school safety, character education, and social service have placed tremendous pressures on school. Learning for all in the second generation goes beyond students to embrace learning for staff, parents, and the community as well. The significant shift in the second generation is from teaching *for* all to learning *by* all.

Safe and Orderly Environment

Creating a settled environment conducive to learning, characterized by the absence of undesirable behaviors, was at the heart of the first generation. The focus was on eliminating elements in the school that would have a negative impact on students and learning.

The second generation focuses on the *presence* of *desirable* behaviors in the school, such as cooperative learning, social justice initiatives, character development, and teamwork for both students and staff. In the second generation, collaboration among staff members serves as a model for students for solving social problems, creating project teams, and mentoring others to create a positive school climate.

Positive Home/School Relations

In the first generation, schools ensured that parents and the community understood and supported the school's basic mission, and that they were given an opportunity to help the school meet its mission.

In the second generation, schools are faced with the fact that social mores have changed, and authority is often challenged. Parents are crucial to school and student success, and paying lip service to them will no longer do. Parents must be included as meaningful partners, and school staff must work to build trusting relationships with parents so that together they can make a positive difference for every student.

Competence Correlates

Embedded in the competence correlates are the knowledge and pedagogical capacity required to ensure learning for all. Ongoing professional learning and skill development are required to ensure that these correlates are strong and readily evident in the work that teachers do with their students.

Climate of High Expectations for Success

In the first generation, the focus was on covering the curriculum. Teachers set goals, taught lessons, and assessed student performance. The assessment strategies were often demanding. In some cases, the high expectations for students were met with high levels of failure. Teachers might give a test and move to the next teaching unit even if some students had been unsuccessful.

In the second generation, the focus shifts to high expectations for teachers to develop strategies that ensure that the high expectations for students are met. Intervention strategies, reteaching, regrouping, mentoring, and tutoring are but some of the methods teachers must use to ensure that high expectations for students are both realistic and attainable.

Frequent Monitoring of Student Progress

In the first generation, students were assessed and the information was used to help students change their behaviors to improve their performance.

In the second generation, because we know more about strategies for achieving improved student performance, the approaches used for monitoring student progress have shifted significantly. While summative assessment (assessment *of* learning) is still seen as important for monitoring achievement at a point in time, formative assessment (assessment *for* and *as* learning) is recognized as a powerful strategy for informing teachers about instructional needs and involving students in their own learning. In the second generation, curriculum is deliberately aligned so that the taught curriculum matches the curriculum that is intended and assessed. Using assessment information, teachers plan instruction and establish structures and procedures to address the needs of all students.

In the second generation, teachers work to answer these questions:

- What is it that students must know?
- Where are they now?
- How must we plan instruction to meet identified learning needs?
- How will we know if students know?
- How will we respond if students do not know or already knew? (DuFour, DuFour, Eaker, & Many, 2006)

Opportunity to Learn and Time on Task

The first generation correlate focused teaching on the essential curriculum, and in it, students would be engaged in whole class or large group, teacher-directed, and planned learning activities most of the time.

The second generation has evolved in response to increased demands on schools to achieve higher results. In it, schools are encouraged to practice *planned abandonment,* a strategy for scaling curriculum back in order to focus on the most essential learning outcomes. Cross-curricular teaching, team teaching, project-based learning, and independent studies are ways to focus instructional time on the most important content and concepts. Authentic or real-world assignments engage students in their learning, and the use of technology enhances time on task. Formative assessment, used effectively, provides teachers with needed information about each student's achievement so the teachers can provide interventions that will give struggling students the extra time on task and additional opportunities to learn they need to ensure success.

Instructional Leadership

Character and competence correlates cannot exist in isolation. Strong instructional leadership demonstrated by teachers and administrators is required to ensure coherence among them.

The Coordinating Correlate

Instructional leadership is the glue that binds the character and competence correlates together. In the first generation, the school administrators were seen as the instructional leaders. They spoke for the school, managed discipline, and monitored teacher performance and student outcomes. They chaired the meetings, set the timetables, and generally supervised the activities in the school. Responsibility for all aspects of student learning and school operation rested squarely on the shoulders of the administrators.

In the second generation, the job of instructional leadership is recognized as being far too big to be managed by two or three people. In the second generation, the ability of administrators to influence students comes through their ability to influence the teachers. The days of compliance, command, and control are behind us. In today's effective schools, the principal is seen as the "lead learner" or "leader of leaders" and realizes that expertise resides in many people, not just one person. School improvement happens in the classrooms, and all staff members are viewed as instructional leaders. The responsibility for leadership in learning belongs to everyone. Teamwork, partnerships, cooperation, and collaboration are the norm for instructional leadership in the second generation. Principals serve as coaches, partners, champions, and cheerleaders.

Strong second generation instructional leadership at the school and district levels is the key to effective, sustained school improvement.

In *Harbors of Hope: The Planning for School and Student Success Process,* we made the point that schools that make a difference for all students are characterized by five qualities:

1. They exhibit the seven correlates of effective schools.

2. They confront the things that interfere with school and student success.

3. They make deliberate plans to improve their school.

4. They use data to inform their planning and monitor their progress.

5. They work within a mindset of continuous improvement.

They recognize that, in schools, things are seldom static. What happens from day to day and year to year represents a constant evolution that informs current needs and actions.

Harbors of Hope

1. Exhibit effective schools correlates.

2. Confront what interferes with school and student success.

3. Plan deliberately.

4. Use data to inform planning and monitor progress.

5. Work within a mindset of continuous improvement.

Planning to Improve

When there is a framework within which to work, planning to improve is much more effective. With this in mind, we presented the Planning for School and Student Success Process (PSSSP) in *Harbors of Hope* as the basis for deliberate planning to improve. True change comes from seeing things in new ways, and the PSSSP articulates five phases to help that happen.

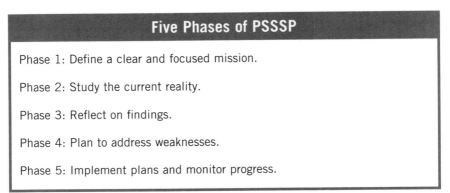

Figure 1-2 ties the five PSSSP phases to the seven correlates of effective schools.

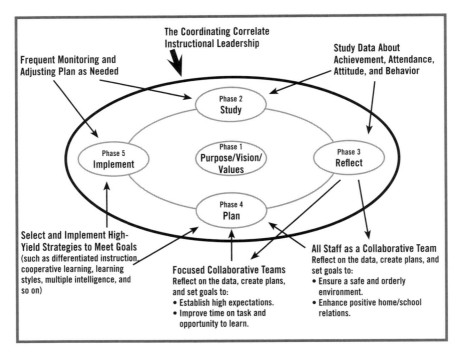

Figure 1-2: The indicators and correlates of effective schools provide the foundation for planning for school and student success.

Our observation is that the PSSSP is a cyclical, self-perpetuating model for continuous and sustained school improvement—a structure to facilitate the reculturing that is necessary to confront what interferes with school and student success. We have worked with teachers and administrators throughout North America to implement the PSSSP and have seen its impact first-hand. It is a user-friendly structure that helps keep thinking focused and provides a framework for critical conversations between teachers, administrators, students, and parents. Over and over again, we have seen that teachers are the key to successful planning to improve. As they work directly with students, they are in the best position to identify existing strengths and areas for improvement. They are the people who are most able to do what is required to improve school and student success.

▶ Teachers are the key to successful planning to improve.

Summary

Through the work we have done since the release of *Harbors of Hope,* our beliefs about schools that make a difference for all students have been confirmed. We have seen Harbors of Hope in action. The mystery of successful planning has been resolved through hearing real stories from real schools. The greatest gift in our work, however, has been that we have continued to learn, and now understand so much more than we did when we wrote *Harbors of Hope,* about what it takes for schools to become places where learning by all is a reality. Chapter 2 outlines the process we have followed in writing this book.

2

Where We Are Now

This book has been motivated by the realization that districts and schools that are moving forward are doing similar things. In a general sense, we knew what those things were; however, we thought that the best way to gain specific understanding would be to consult the experts—those people in the field who are working daily to create and sustain schools that are Harbors of Hope. We knew they would have stories to tell and strategies to share.

With that in mind, we contacted people we have worked with to seek their support for our field research. Our consultation has taken us into 21 school districts in seven Canadian provinces. Initially, our superintendent and director colleagues assisted us by recommending schools in their districts that:

1. Could provide data that validate improved learning results

2. Could identify specific strategies that can be traced to improved results

3. Have developed a positive collaborative culture

4. Have made the development of teacher leadership capacity a priority

We approached the identified schools to invite their involvement. To begin the process, we asked the principals to provide us with information on the four identified criteria. We also developed a four-point rubric for each of the criteria, which we sent out to the schools to inform them about how we would be reviewing their materials (see appendix A, page 207). We received 45 submissions and were delighted with the overall response. The material we received from the schools validated our thinking that the criteria we identified are, in fact, the keys to successful schools. See appendix B, page 211, for the list of schools that provided the data behind this book.

Once we had the submissions from the schools, we began the task of reading and sorting. We recognized that we had more information than we could hope to use effectively and knew we would need to reduce the number of schools involved and gather additional information from those that we identified for further research. In the second round of data collection, we asked for more specific and detailed information about school profiles, data used to validate improvement, specific actions taken in response to what the data indicated, and challenges faced and solutions found. Again, we were delighted with the response.

Armed with still more information, we combed through the material to look for trends that would answer our questions about what improving schools do to make a difference for all students. As necessary, we contacted participating schools personally to seek additional clarification and learn more about the journeys being shared with us. Along the way, many principals also contacted us to provide new information as it was discovered.

Our work with the schools has been informative and exciting—gratifying in many ways. We have continued to learn from these talented, committed educators who have so generously shared their data, their time, and their stories. All of the schools are at different places on the school improvement journey, but they are all definitely on it. All are moving forward, and all can look back over past years to demonstrate that their schools are improving and all students are learning. Some have been at it longer than others and, as a result, are further along in the journey. Some do not yet have all of the data they need to demonstrate conclusively that their improvement efforts are paying dividends. What they do know, however, is that they are seeing growth. For most, the charted progress from year to year looks more like a wavy line than a dramatic upward trend. However, when asked, "Are your school and students demonstrating greater success this year than last?" they can all answer, "Yes." All have the evidence to substantiate their claim and can highlight the actions that supported the improvement.

> Successful schools, when asked, "Are your school and students demonstrating greater success this year than last?" are all able to answer, "Yes"—and all have the evidence to substantiate their claim.

These schools exhibit proactive, hopeful thinking, and they recognize that the improvement journey is a perpetual process that continues from year to year, with the work of each year building on what was done the year before. All of the schools measure their progress frequently by looking back at where they have been and ahead to where they want to go. All have clearly defined goals for improvement that reflect the values that are evident within the staff. In all of them, the second generation correlates of effective schools are evident, and learning for all is clearly the overarching purpose for everything they do.

Seven Lessons, Seven Correlates

We have been struck with the congruity among the schools included in our research, although each one is unique. They all exhibit seven common themes that we are calling "lessons for school success." All have improved as a result of successfully incorporating these lessons into the culture of their school. At the heart of each lesson lies the second generation of the seven effective schools correlates; one or two of the correlates is particularly prominent in each lesson.

Lesson One: School Change Is Difficult . . . Expect It to Be Messy and Upsetting

Changing the culture of any organization is difficult, but schools are exceptional challenges. By nature and design, they are conservative places in which radical change is not acceptable. Many parents do not want schools to change to influence the future, but would prefer to turn the clocks back to the "good old days." Change will cause upset. Senior administrators and elected officials may not be pleased to hear about upset. Schools have historically been sorting places where student futures are determined by academic success; therefore, school improvement and change often meet resistance on many fronts. The process of shifting a school's culture requires vision, tenacious commitment to creating a better future for kids, and the courage to do whatever it takes.

▶ The prominent correlate: Clear and focused mission

Lesson Two: Leadership Matters . . . The More the Better

Leadership is about influence—the ability to conceive of a big picture and work with people to bring it to fruition. While formal leadership is critical to school planning success, it is not sufficient. Informal leadership capacity must also be developed and distributed throughout the staff. Teachers are viewed as leaders of learning, while administrators are leaders of leaders.

The prominent correlate: Instructional leadership (at the school level)

Lesson Three: Measurement Matters . . . But Not to Everyone

In *Harbors of Hope* (Hulley & Dier, 2005), we made the point that planning that is not based on data is "planning to plan" as opposed to "planning to improve." The focus in planning to plan is on implementing new programs, strategies, and activities. A plan to *improve,* however, is based on meaningful data or critical evidence about student achievement and overall school success in terms of providing a climate and environment conducive to optimal learning. Based on what the critical evidence indicates, clear goals are established that, when achieved, will be evidence that improvement has occurred. Teachers may view the use of data negatively and with suspicion. The fact is, however, that change and improvement are impossible to track and validate without it. There are different kinds of data and many different sources for it. The challenge is to determine which critical evidence or data is most meaningful. Planning to improve revolves around engaging staff in collecting, organizing, and analyzing critical evidence in order to improve their practice.

 The prominent correlate: Frequent monitoring of student progress

Lesson Four: If at First You Don't Succeed . . . Do Whatever It Takes

Good ideas and theory are not necessarily foolproof. Even the most carefully crafted plans can contain stumbling blocks and take longer than expected to yield results. This can be discouraging and frustrating to the people who are working hard to implement those plans. People may be tempted to give up and revert to old ways because they are familiar—even though they may not be effective. Change takes time, effort, and support. Collaborative teams setting goals, celebrating small victories, and making "in-flight corrections" when there are problems are the key to keeping change initiatives alive and moving forward.

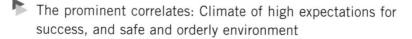 The prominent correlates: Climate of high expectations for success, and safe and orderly environment

Lesson Five: Getting It Right Once Is Not Enough . . . Growth and Learning Must Be Ongoing

As educators, we have a responsibility to help all students learn by providing them with the opportunities to learn and time on task they need to be successful. To do this, we must be committed to continual reflection on the impact of our work and be prepared to make adjustments when we are not achieving success. Teachers, like their students, also need opportunities and time to learn. Sometimes the parent community also needs time and opportunity to learn. To be effective, learning and growth for *all* must be focused and ongoing.

▶ The prominent correlate: Opportunity to learn and time on task

Lesson Six: Academics Are the Focus . . . But Other Things Matter, Too

Learning in schools is both curricular and personal. Academic achievement is essential. So is personal and interpersonal growth. Our world is increasingly diverse, and the implications of this are significant. It is imperative that we create school climates that support the risk-taking required for both students and teachers to acquire the academic, personal, and teamwork skills that are critical for the future. Because parents and the community at large are significant stakeholders in the education of today's children and youth, it is important to enlist them as partners in order to support all kinds of learning.

▶ The prominent correlate: Positive home/school relations

Lesson Seven: Expect Rocks and Hard Places . . . They Are Inevitable

In Lesson 2, the focus is on instructional leadership at the *school* level and the importance of developing leadership capacity in all staff so leadership responsibility can be shared. Lesson 7 focuses on instructional leadership at the *system* level and what it means to be aligned. It is possible for individual schools to make significant gains working independently; however, when the entire district is aligned, the ability of each school to move forward and the likelihood of success will be greatly enhanced. Because planning to improve necessitates change, and change challenges the old and understood ways of operating, we can be assured that conflict and problems will surface.

Rocks and hard places are inevitable. Strong instructional leadership at the *district* level can have a significant impact on reducing barriers to change.

 The prominent correlate: Instructional leadership (this time at the division level)

Summary

All the schools that have worked with us are wonderful examples of Harbors of Hope. All illustrate the seven lessons we have identified as well as the second generation of correlates at work. Our goal has been to represent them fairly and tell their stories in a way that is practical and meaningful for our readers. Section 2 is organized according to the seven lessons for school success and the effective schools correlate(s) that are prominent within them. Each lesson is identified and described, citing research. Descriptive stories from the real world are included in each lesson.

Lessons for School Success

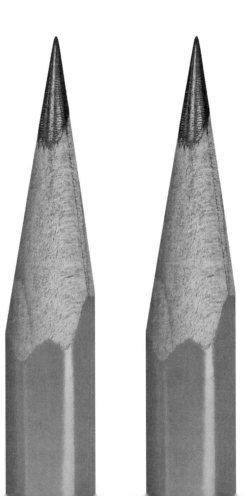

School Change Is Difficult . . . Expect It to Be Messy and Upsetting

Most teachers are caring, committed professionals who are doing what they believe is right. At the suggestion of change, there is a natural tendency to resist because most people are comfortable with the status quo—the way things have always been done. The first reaction might be, "It's not broken, so why are we trying to fix it?" The fact is, there is always room for growth, and learning is never complete.

To build commitment to the improvement process, it is necessary for educators to spend time reflecting and talking about the school they want to create and articulating the values they will have to live in order for that to happen. Often it is the principal, initially, who holds the vision for the school's future; however, when teachers are given time and structured opportunities to understand, add to, and endorse the new vision and values, the chances of achieving the vision are enhanced. Change is a process, not an event. It will never be smooth because everyone adopts change at a different rate. Without structured conversations and tangible support, personal commitment to change will be elusive, and the process will be impeded.

The Link to Effective Schools Research

The "clear and focused mission" correlate is prominent in this lesson. In an effective school, staff members share a clearly articulated mission or purpose that answers the question, "What does this school care most about?" When staff members understand and share a commitment to school goals and priorities, they also share the responsibility for them. Lezotte and McKee (2002) concluded that "the more we work with schools and the more we visit a variety of schools, the more we become convinced that the issue of mission is one that must receive substantial discussion" (p. 17).

The work encompassed in addressing this correlate is sometimes viewed as "navel gazing" and is discounted as being too vague and time-consuming to warrant the attention of busy educators. Taking this view is a mistake. The scope of teaching is enormous, presenting an endless array of possibilities for initiatives that might be undertaken in an effort to improve a school. Time and energy are finite; therefore, it is imperative that improvement efforts be specific and focused if they are to have a positive impact on school and student success. With a clear and shared sense of mission or purpose, the efforts of staff members can be refined and directed at determining what must be accomplished, and then doing what is required to make it happen.

> In schools that are Harbors of Hope, learning by all is a reality. In these schools, the correlates work in concert and are interdependent. All seven are consistently present and powerfully demonstrated.

What We Have Learned About the Lesson

In our work, we have encountered many approaches to school planning ranging from an urgent acknowledgement that there is much room for improvement to complacency born of the belief that "we are already successful and do not need to think about improvement." Our belief is that the school a student attends matters. Our experience has been that no matter how successful a school is, there is always room for growth and improvement. If even one student in a school or district is not experiencing success, there is room for improvement, and changes must be made to find ways to address it.

There are many challenges inherent in the change process; therefore, it is critical that those who will be affected by it be involved from the beginning in a process of identifying the beliefs, values, and purposes that they share. The final product (written statements of beliefs, vision, and purpose) is just words. The value is in the *process* of developing the statements, because that is what engages the hearts and minds of the participants. Everyone involved must have the opportunity to be heard by others and to understand the views of their colleagues.

Conversations of this sort engage emotions and intellect because they strike at the core of what it means to be a good teacher. As people work together to identify the beliefs they hold in common and develop the combined vision of the future they want to create, a foundation of shared purpose is built that serves as a touchstone to guide all subsequent work. Such a process goes a long way toward creating a collegial climate that supports a community of learners with the capacity to incorporate new ideas, critically assess outcomes, and use measurable results to gauge progress. Frequent reviews of shared beliefs, vision, and purpose serve to refresh and reaffirm commitments. They provide a standard against which to gauge progress in school improvement work.

Assessing the Current Culture

For a school to become a Harbor of Hope, staff members must commit to making learning for *all* the priority in their school. With commitment comes the responsibility to assess the school's current culture carefully to ascertain if learning for all is, in fact, the main event. Staff members must ask themselves: Is our school climate conducive to learning? Are relationships between students, teachers, and parents strong and based on trust? Are we using the best possible strategies for teaching and learning? Are all of our students experiencing success through making satisfactory progress? Are we continuing to grow professionally, individually, and as a group? Doing the research to find the answers to these and other questions, as well as collecting critical evidence to substantiate the answers, is the key to accurately assessing the school's current culture.

 In a Harbor of Hope, the culture ensures that learning for *all* is the main event.

Educators can get a sense of a school's culture formally, by gathering feedback about the school from the members of the school community, and informally, by observing the interactions of teachers with each other, with students, and with other adults in the building. The condition of the hallways and classrooms speaks volumes. Are they bright and clean? Is there evidence of student work and school pride? The most telling clues are how teachers talk about students; what they expect of them; and what their achievement scores show. When teachers and other staff take an honest look at their current reality, they will be able to identify areas of strength as well as areas that interfere with optimal school and student success. Jim Collins (2001) called this "confronting the brutal facts" (p. 32).

In *Good to Great and the Social Sectors* (2005), Collins wrote of factors that detract from confronting the brutal facts within social sectors. He identified cultures of niceness that "inhibit candor about the brutal facts" and spoke of systemic constraints that can "erode faith in the ability to prevail in the end" (p. 32). His position, however, is that rather than waiting for the system to be fixed, groups of committed people can, in fact, build pockets of greatness within it. In confronting the brutal facts, the aim is to answer the question, "Do we really make learning for all a priority?" If the answer is not an unqualified yes, there is a clear mandate that the culture of the school must shift. Change must occur.

Understanding Change

One of the most complicated issues with which educators wrestle in the school improvement process is how to understand the change process. Change, by definition, disturbs the status quo. No one is exempt from its impact. It is a lengthy process during which cultural and social identities are challenged. Everyone involved is forced outside of their comfort zone and required to adapt to new professional and personal challenges. People react to the prospect of change in different ways. Some actively seek and initiate it, seeming to thrive on change. Others proceed cautiously as they prepare to tackle new things. Still others are skeptical and will search for ways to avoid it. Change is a complex process that requires understanding and knowledge in order to effectively see it through.

Michael Fullan (2001) asserted that change "cannot be managed. It can be understood and perhaps led, but it cannot be controlled" (p. 33); Fullan also reports the belief of Mintzberg, Ahlstrand, and Lampel (1998) that "the best way to 'manage' change is to allow for it to happen. . . . To be pulled by the concerns out there rather than being pushed by the concepts in here" (Fullan, 2001, p. 373). In other words, change initiatives are best developed and led by the people who will be working on them. In schools, those people are the teachers, caring people who, by virtue of being closely connected to students, are in the best position to see possibilities, identify things that could be improved, and lead the change process.

> ▶ Teachers are in the best position to see possibilities, identify things that could be improved, and lead the change process.

The process of change is not immediate, nor is it linear. It is likely to emerge over 3 to 5 years and involve a lot of angst along the way as people struggle to alter their perspectives and take the risks required to assimilate new learning. Because it disturbs the status quo, change is messy; and messiness is more upsetting for some people than for others. It is inherent in the creative process and the search for solutions to thorny problems that do not have easy answers. Heifetz and Linsky (2002) referred to these thorny problems as "adaptive challenges" and compared them to technical issues for which solutions are already known. They told us that we know we are dealing with an adaptive challenge when "people's hearts and minds need to change, and not just their preferences or routine behaviors" (p. 60). To address an adaptive challenge, "People have to learn new ways . . . and cultures must distinguish what is essential from what is expendable as they move forward" (p. 60). As change begins to occur, the climate can feel chaotic. The comfort of what is known and understood is gone, and knowledge of what lies ahead is, at best, sketchy. People will respond based on their tolerance for ambivalence and the risk-taking that is part of the change process.

Everett Rogers (2003) put forward a *diffusion of innovations theory* that helps us to understand various reactions to change. Rogers describes diffusion as the process by which an innovation (change) is communicated over time among members of a social system. He maintained that how people perceive an innovation in terms of its relative advantage and their ability to manage it is determined by the rate at which they would adopt it. Rogers suggested that people affected by a change would typically fall into one of five adopter categories:

1. Innovators (risk-takers)

2. Early adopters (hedgers)

3. Early majority (waiters)

4. Late majority (skeptics)

5. Late adopters (slowpokes)

The different rates of adoption have a significant impact on the path an innovation takes. People who adjust easily to change are often frustrated by those who are slower to adjust. At the same time, those who are slower to change can be aggravated by those who are eager and enthusiastic. Therein lays a significant component of the challenge inherent in the change process. It is important to realize that while innovators and early adopters tend to begin the process, the ultimate gauge of success is the extent of buy-in from majority and late adopters.

The *concerns-based adoption model (CBAM)* of change complements Rogers' diffusion of innovations theory and provides strategies to assist educators in supporting staff in various adopter categories through change. Originally developed by Hall and Hord (1987), this model has been well-researched and further developed by many respected educators who have found useful applications for it in different arenas. The CBAM explores how people approach change and the typical path they follow as they work toward adopting an innovation. In Figure 3-1, Sweeny (2003) depicts human learning and development as going through seven stages during which a person's focus or concern shifts in predictable ways.

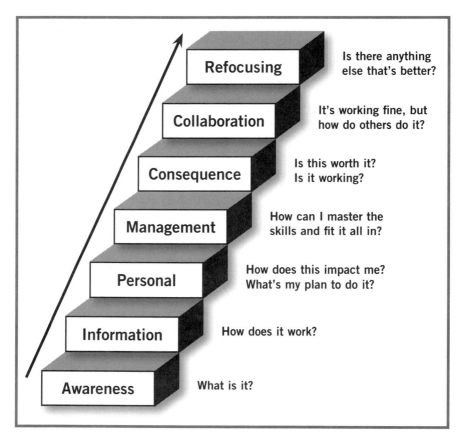

Figure 3-1: The concerns-based adoption model: The seven stages of concern

From "The CBAM: A Model of the People Development Process," by B. Sweeny (2003). Copyright Barry Sweeny. Accessed at http://www.mentoring-association.org/membersonly/ CBAM.html on December 13, 2007. Adapted from a diagram in G. Hall & S. Hord, *Taking Charge of Change* (1987). Alexandria, VA: Association for Supervision and Curriculum Development. Reprinted with permission.

Note that questions in the early stages of concern are primarily self-oriented, as people consider the innovation and what it means for them personally. Once those concerns are resolved, more task-oriented questions emerge. When self and task concerns have been addressed, people can focus on the impact of the change being made. As educators, the questions revolve around how well this change is working for students and whether there is something else that would work even better. As people refocus at the last stage and ponder what that something else might be, the journey through the stages begins again. While the model looks linear, it is, in fact, cyclical. The strength of the CBAM model is in its reminder to pay attention to individuals and their need for information, assistance, and moral support. It is those things that affect the rate of adoption of any new innovation.

Fullan and Steigelbauer (1991) further developed the CBAM model by extending its application to focus on leading change efforts from a variety of perspectives. They recognized that adopter concerns evolve over time, in different settings, and in different ways depending upon the person's role. They identified eight such roles or stakeholder groups to consider in any change process: students, teachers, parents and community, school administrators, district administrators, consultants, teacher educators, and policymakers. Fullan and Steigelbauer emphasize assessing and understanding the various perspectives and strategies for building coalitions, and then identifying common goals for those whose collaboration is needed or those who may resist the desired change.

Eight Stakeholder Groups to Consider in the Change Process

1. Students

2. Teachers

3. Parents and community

4. School administrators

5. District administrators

6. Consultants

7. Teacher educators

8. Policymakers

(Adapted from Fullan & Steigelbauer, 1991)

Responding to Change

When we are asked to rethink what we believe and how we work, we feel loss. Old habits do die hard, because the acquisition of new habits demands that we give up familiar practices, live with uncertainty, and risk failure as we learn. Even if we know that change is necessary, there is no guarantee that the change will be an improvement.

William Bridges (1991) tells us that "it isn't the changes that do you in, it's the transitions" (p. 1). Resistance is an effort to restore equilibrium by shutting down those who are leading the change efforts. Heifetz and Linsky (2002) identified four different forms of resistance that leaders may be forced to handle. They indicated that there were innumerable creative manifestations of each:

1. **Marginalization.** Being sidelined or ostracized; the effect of this can be felt by people who are leading the change as well as those who are supporting it.

2. **Diversion.** Being faced with a myriad of distractions and as a result, being unable to focus on the change effort in question

3. **Attack.** Being criticized about the initiative, personal character, or style

4. **Seduction.** Being drawn in by the desire for approval or reluctance to disappoint those who have been supporters in the past and, as a result, losing the sense of purpose for the change

Resistance to change is inevitable. The degree to which it is manifested will vary according to people's ability and willingness to deal with the change. Even innovators and early adopters are not immune to feelings of resistance as their competence is challenged and they deal with the uncertainty of change. Everyone is susceptible, and as the change unfolds, there is likely to be frustration and conflict as people struggle to understand each other's perspectives. Risk-takers and slowpokes do not necessarily relate well to one another! Kotter (1996) summed it up this way:

> Change zealots tend to demonize resisters, but they are not really bad people. Like all of us, they are a product of their history. They have had experiences that have led to the adoption of certain deeply ingrained behaviours and habits. The best solution is usually honest dialogue. (p. 112)

Not all resistance is overt. Do not consider an apparent absence of resistance a good omen. In fact, if there is no resistance, chances are that little significant change is occurring. Lack of resistance may be an indication that the wrapper has changed—but what is in the box is still the same. At best, it may be an indication of indifference; at worst, it may be a manifestation of subversion. To ignore resistance (or its absence) is a mistake because it will inevitably surface and have a negative impact on the work being done to make changes. It is the *degree* of resistance that determines the extent of its impact on the change process and how it must be addressed. Is resistance easy to deal with? No. Is it critical that it be dealt with? Absolutely!

▶ Lack of resistance may be an indication that the wrapper has changed—but what is in the box is still the same.

Human nature being what it is, we all gravitate toward people who think like us and tend to avoid or discount those who do not. Fullan (2001) suggested that we ought to appreciate resistance and view it as a "potential source of new ideas and breakthroughs" (p. 74). In fact, we are more likely to learn something new or see things through different lenses when we talk with those who do not see things exactly as we do. It is easier to deal with resistance when the work has been done to articulate shared beliefs, vision, and purpose, and teamwork is facilitated within a climate of respectful interaction that recognizes the gifts that are inherent in diverse ways of thinking.

▶ It is easier to deal with resistance when the work has been done to articulate shared beliefs, vision, and purpose, and teamwork is facilitated within a climate of open, respectful interaction.

Most often, resistance can be addressed through discussion, joint planning, and tangible support for new learning. Sometimes, however, it cannot. Collins (2005) identified the good-to-great concept of "getting the right people on the bus—in the right seats," and he spoke to the difficulty of getting the wrong people off the bus in the social sectors. He stressed the importance of early assessment systems and learning supports for new hires in order to ensure that tenure is granted only to those teachers who love kids and are passionate about making a difference for them.

Some people show resistance because the change being sought is completely beyond their ability to fathom or adapt at a given point in time. When that is the case, they may have to move to another spot that is better suited for their existing stage of development as a teacher. Resistance emanating from people for whom teaching is just a job and for whom moral purpose and passion for working with children and youth simply do not exist is a different issue. In these instances, the importance of administrative intervention and personal contracting for change cannot be overstated. People who cannot overcome resistance to the changes being sought are not unworthy people. They may simply be in the wrong seat on the bus or on the wrong bus altogether!

 Resistance emanating from people for whom teaching is just a job and for whom moral purpose and passion for working with children and youth simply do not exist must be addressed.

What the Lesson Teaches Us

- At first, the principal may be the only person with the vision; however, through reflection and thoughtful conversation, that vision can be shared by all.

- Change efforts are most successful when they are guided by a strong vision and shared purpose.

- A positive school culture encourages commitment.

- Change initiatives are best developed and led by the people who will be working on them.

- A well-thought-out action plan that is understood by all is critical to the success of change initiatives.

- The change process is messy and nonlinear. Frustration, conflict, and resistance are inevitable and must be addressed.

- Change requires that people step outside of their comfort zone to learn new things. New learning challenges peoples' feelings of competence. Expect people to be confused and upset as they struggle to feel confident again.

- Support, training, resources, and incentives are required to facilitate change efforts.

- Threats and punishments will not help.

- Strong, differentiated leadership is imperative.

- Change is a process, not an event. Expect to take 3–5 years to fully address concerns and embed the change in the culture of the school.

Lessons Lived: A Story From the Real World

What follows is a story about change and the inspired leadership of the principal who led the process. At first it was the principal's vision that was fueling the process. In the final analysis, the vision was shared by all and was reflected in the daily work of the school.

Valley Farm Public School

Valley Farm Public School (VFPS) is located in a highly diverse community in the city of Pickering, Ontario. There are over 35 different cultures evident in the school. The Board of Education made VFPS a priority school based on longitudinal results from the Ontario Education Quality and Accountability Office (EQAO). Driving into the school area, one would not suspect the extent of needs that exist within it. Houses are large and for the most part well-kept. The fact is, however, that many of the houses are home to multiple families—one to each bedroom, with the garage being used as the family room. Gang activity, drug operations, and other issues in the neighborhood require regular police presence.

The staff of Valley Farm Public School consists of 36.8 staff members, including two and a half special education resource teachers, a principal, and a vice principal. Eight of the staff members have over 10 years of experience, and 16 have less than 2 years experience. There are four male teachers and 32.8 female teachers. The school serves students from junior kindergarten through grade 8. There are three classes at each grade level as well as combined classes of grades 2 and 3, grades 3 and 4, and grades 6 and 7. Until 2005, grades 3 to 6 were housed in portable facilities.

Since 2001, the enrollment at VFPS has declined from 755 to 654 students, of whom 355 are female and 299 are male. Sixty-one students are identified as having special needs. All but nine of them are integrated into regular classrooms. Those children are taught in special education classrooms. Twenty-two students in grades 4 through 6 are identified as being at risk because of low self-esteem, poor academic achievement, police involvement, and dysfunctional attitudes and behaviors. The English-language learner (also known as English as a Second Language [ELL or ESL]) population is growing quickly, with the majority of students coming from Pakistan, Afghanistan, Iraq, and India. Most of these students arrive in Canada with no English and limited schooling. Many East Indian families take their children out of school for up to 3 months during the school year to make extended trips back home. Transience is an issue as well. It is not unusual for 30–40 students to move out of the school in a month and a new group of 30–40 students to arrive in the same month.

Getting Started

Silvia Peterson arrived at the school in 2001 and faced many challenges as the new principal. Initially, she found that the culture of the school was influenced by a prevailing belief that weak students, unsupportive parents, and low socioeconomic status made it impossible to expect academic achievement. Silvia recognized that there was a need to focus on specific curriculum areas and initiatives. She also identified the need for alignment and agreement among staff members regarding policies, structures, and practices. A common vision and long-range planning were necessary to guide their work into the future.

The staff was divided and unsure about what to expect from their new administrator. Many staff members were comfortable with past practices and saw no need to do things differently. Now, with a new administration and changed expectations, they were being asked to step outside of their comfort zone to think and work differently. It was no surprise that Silvia encountered resistance. She knew that she had her work cut out for her if she was going to be successful in guiding the reculturing process that was necessary to make learning for all a priority at VFPS.

Silvia began by sharing her vision, her high expectations for staff and students, and her commitment to being the principal of the school. She spoke passionately about student failure not being an option and her desire to build a team that would support the learning and success of all.

Providing Structures, Supports, and Incentives

Although many teachers did not share her vision, Silvia did not give up. Instead, she focused on developing collaborative relationships with those who did. She worked deliberately to provide opportunity, support, and incentives for those teachers who were willing to become involved in the work of the school.

Silvia created division chair positions for primary, junior, and intermediate divisions. At each grade, she chose a lead teacher to meet weekly with his or her grade-level colleagues to discuss students and learning. Division chairs met monthly with their divisions to do the following:

• Focus on student achievement in literacy and numeracy.

- Seek solutions to concerns about students.

- Plan field trips, special events, and excursions.

- Plan celebrations.

The school established task forces (committees) for literacy, numeracy, safe schools, and student success. Silvia chose a chairperson for each task force and invited teachers to join a task force of their choice. The mandate of each task force was to assess the school's achievement in the identified areas. Members analyzed data looking for comparisons, patterns, and trends. They interpreted their findings and shared them with the entire staff. All teachers had input at staff meetings and division meetings. Ultimately, the task forces considered all of the input and devised a plan of action that included goals, strategies, indicators of success, and methods of monitoring. They also identified resources and professional development opportunities that were needed.

In the early years of Silvia's tenure, membership in the task forces was very low. Those teachers who did not share the vision and high expectations continued to resist Silvia and what she was trying to do. Between 2002 and 2003, however, membership in the task forces rose steadily as staff learned that, in fact, these committees were driving the school plan. Teachers realized that if they wanted to have influence, they would have to become involved in the life of the school. By the end of the 2003 school year, many of the teachers who could not or would not share in the school's vision had left the school, and things looked quite different at VFPS. Silvia had worked diligently to empower and involve teachers, develop a cohesive team, and build capacity for leading and learning. She was starting to see results.

Sharing Leadership and Planning to Improve

A school improvement team was created that included division chairs, lead teachers from each grade, special education resource teachers, the teacher-librarian, the computer site administrator, and the school's administrative team. This team meets monthly to plan the school budget and allocation of funds, school-based professional development activities, and staff meetings and to collate the overall school plan. The school improvement team reviews the plans created by the task forces to ensure that they are realistic and feasible for inclusion in the overall school plan. Once finalized, the school plan is distributed and discussed with the entire staff. It is reviewed twice each term to ensure that it is on track. Planning for next year begins in the spring, and by the end of May each year, the staff knows the direction for the year ahead.

Committing to Credible, Proactive Leadership

As she worked with the staff of VFPS, Silvia was committed to building credibility with teachers and parents alike by openly sharing information about budget, curriculum, and upcoming initiatives that would affect them. Through newsletters, announcements, and personal notes, she made a conscious effort to highlight the good things that were happening at the school. She made it a priority to recognize staff for their efforts and celebrate their achievements. She also made a point of showcasing her staff and their good work through School Community Council meetings and presentations to the Board of Education.

From the beginning, Silvia's expectations for teachers were high, and she supported them through providing time to work together, information to help them understand the expectations, training to acquire needed skills, and the resources they needed to be successful. She was very clear about failure not being an option and the importance of using the curriculum to teach *children,* not just *content.* Silvia identified literacy and numeracy as focal points and emphasized Ministry and Board policies to promote understanding and consistency. A baseline assessment program was implemented at all grades to collect critical evidence about student achievement levels and growth three times a year. Teachers used templates they were provided for long-range planning, daybooks, and communication logs. They were expected to work together by grade to:

- Create data walls to show levels and growth for all students at each grade level.

- Create class profiles that identify individual student strengths and learning needs.

- Work monthly with the Board facilitators on literacy and numeracy to conduct action research on new strategies for instruction.

- Identify common curricular outcomes.

- Develop common assignments and assessments.

- Develop rubrics, share marking, and examine student work together.

- Select common expectations to be included on the report card.

- Create templates for communication with parents.

Making Continuous Growth a Priority

Silvia revamped staff meetings to focus on professional development. She provided professional reading to stimulate discussion and new learning. As much as possible, teachers were encouraged to attend conferences and in-service sessions together—as a team. Silvia often invited teachers to attend in-services with her and then to return to the school and present, together, what they had learned. Fees for any or all teachers wishing to attend professional development sessions based on the school plan during the Board's Summer Institutes were paid for through block funding.

Knowing that time is always an issue for teachers, Silvia was determined to find ways to create time for them to work together. Common prep time for teachers at VFPS is the norm. In addition, each division is released for approximately 90 minutes once a month during the instructional day to be engaged in professional development with Board facilitators on literacy and numeracy. To provide that time, the principal and vice principal, along with some support staff, take the students into the gym to work on character education. Division chairs are also released for a half day each term to meet and work with the administration on divisional issues. Members of the school improvement team are also released monthly to join the administrative team for discussions about the progress of school improvement plans.

Looking Back With Satisfaction

For 5½ years, Silvia was part of an impressive transformation at VFPS. Silvia was passionate about her vision and communicated it consistently. She did not allow herself to be distracted from it or become intimidated by the significant resistance she experienced at the outset. Instead, she systematically developed staff capacity by providing them with skills, resources, and incentives. She listened intently and involved the teachers in making decisions and developing plans for their school. In the final analysis, she was instrumental in building a strong, collaborative team of leaders. In February 2007, when Silvia was transferred to another school, she referred to the staff of VFPS as her dream team and said, "You couldn't find a better staff anywhere!"

In 2007, Valley Farm Public School was on the short list for a Garfield Weston Award for Excellence in Education in the category of "Improvement in Academics." Based on the Annual Report Cards on Ontario's Elementary Schools, the Fraser Institute identifies schools that represent the top 1% of Ontario's schools in each award area and invites them to participate.

"Improvement in Academics" recognizes the school team whose overall academic rating has experienced the fastest, most consistent improvement over the previous 5 years.

Summary

Change is difficult. We can expect it to be messy and upsetting because it shifts the culture of the school. Because change is so complicated, the change process must be well-understood and treated with respect. A clear and focused mission that is understood and shared by all provides the foundation for the work to be done. When people begin to work differently, the school's culture has successfully shifted.

For the change process to unfold effectively, it is important to attend to where people are currently and address their questions *before* expecting them to do things differently. Moving to action before addressing concerns is counterproductive. On the other hand, talking and addressing concerns for a prolonged period blocks progress and serves as a form of resistance. There comes a time when schools need to take the plunge. New approaches to teaching require practice, and they often bring surprises that result in further new learning. Support over time is necessary to work out the kinks and reinforce good teaching. Things like professional development opportunities, access to new resources, release time for planning, and involvement on decision-making committees provide incentives for teachers to embrace the change process. When the inevitable resistance surfaces, it must be acknowledged and addressed—never ignored.

These are exciting times to be involved in education; however, they are not without conflict. Conflict is what we make of it. The Chinese ideogram for conflict contains two characters: One means "danger" and the other "hidden opportunity." Reculturing takes time. It demands incredible commitment and tenacity on the part of the people involved. Initiative fatigue and frustration are inevitable and can take their toll as people learn and try new approaches to the important work they are doing. It falls to leaders to uncover the hidden opportunities inherent in the change process and to keep it moving forward. Chapter 4 focuses on leadership at the school level, the second lesson for school success.

Leadership Matters . . .
The More, the Better

Leadership is about influence. It is about having a vision of a better future for students and staff. It is also about passion, moral purpose, and commitment to learning for all. Strong administrative leadership based on clearly communicated beliefs and values is critical to school improvement success, but it is not sufficient. School administrators today are expected to be visionary. They should be able to inspire passion and a sense of moral purpose in their staff. They are expected to be excellent managers of budget and plant-related issues—as well as instructional leaders who are knowledgeable about curriculum and best instructional practices. Demands from multiple stakeholders and accountability requirements further compound the expectations placed on them. The amount of work to be done is enormous and complex. It commands far more expertise and energy than could ever be provided by only those who hold formal administrative titles. To be effective, leadership needs to be shared.

Teachers are naturally the leaders in their classrooms; however, they also have the potential to be significant leaders at the school and district levels because they know firsthand what is needed to improve student learning. When teachers take an active role in the improvement of school or districtwide policies and programs, leadership is distributed among many people, each leading in his or her own way based on a vision that is shared. Therefore, creating cultures that support teacher leadership is a priority. Opportunities must be provided for teachers to develop and practice their leadership skills.

▶ To be effective, leadership needs to be shared.

The Link to Effective Schools Research

The prominent correlate for this lesson is "instructional leadership," with the focus at the school level. In effective schools, the principal sets the precedent of identifying shared values and priorities. Once they have been articulated, the principal's primary goal is to keep them at the forefront as reminders of the standards that have been chosen to guide the work of staff, parents, and students. Note that in the second generation of this correlate, teachers are central to attainment of the values and priorities that have been identified. Because of this, they must also be recognized as instructional leaders in the school. Administrators must shift to being leaders of leaders intent on guiding, supporting, and empowering teachers. Teachers must come to the fore as leaders in pursuit of the mission of learning for all.

Lezotte and McKee (2002) told us that principals need to be proactive, interactive, and reactive. They must proactively "seize on every chance that comes along to remind teachers, parents, support staff and students themselves of the school's mission" (p. 164). While working with and supporting teachers as they strive to ensure student mastery of essential outcomes, principals must "invest as much time and energy as is realistically possible in the place where the mission of learning meets the road—the classroom" (p. 164). Reactively speaking, they must "focus as much of the organizational energy as is feasible on the data that indicate the extent to which the school is achieving its mission" (p. 164).

> In schools that are Harbors of Hope, learning by all is a reality. In these schools, the correlates work in concert and are interdependent. All seven are consistently present and powerfully demonstrated.

What We Have Learned About the Lesson

According to Marzano (2003), leadership is the single most important aspect of effective school reform. Fullan (2005) supported this position and went further to tell us that "leadership is to this decade what standards-based reform was to the 1990s" (p. xi). He encouraged us to think in terms of *leadership,* as opposed to *leaders.* He suggested that the "main mark of an effective principal is not just his or her impact on the bottom line of student achievement, but also on how many good leaders he or she leaves behind who can go even further" (p. 35). To leave a truly lasting legacy, administrators must ensure that teacher leadership dispositions and skills are developed, honed, and practiced long before they assume their first full-time, formal positions of authority.

The Importance of Administrative Leadership

While shared leadership is the ultimate goal, the fact remains that substantive and sustained school improvement begins with the school principal. Effective leaders need a multifaceted collection of skills, understandings, and dispositions; however, their priority must be relationship-building. Solid relationships are the prerequisite for successful leadership. Relationships are so critically important because they are governed by emotion, and emotion is more forceful than intellect. Strong emotion can powerfully affect our ability to think rationally. Effective leaders recognize the impact of emotions (both their own and those of others) and understand the importance of a well-developed understanding of emotional intelligence.

 Substantive and sustained school improvement begins with the school principal.

Goleman, Boyatzis, and McKee (2002) identified four aspects of emotional intelligence:

1. Emotional self-awareness

2. Emotional self-management

3. Awareness of others' emotions (empathy)

4. Managing relationships with others

They concluded that when all four of these aspects of emotional intelligence are well-developed, people *resonate*—they are self-aware and able to manage their own emotions. In addition, because they are equipped to understand and deal with the emotions of others, they have the skills to deal with issues rather than burying them. Astute leaders focus on developing their own emotional intelligence while helping others develop theirs. They lead from clearly articulated statements of personal values, priorities, purpose, and goals, and in the process, they connect with those held by others in order to arrive at a vision and purpose that are shared by all.

Goleman spoke of resonant teams, saying that all teams or groups have a mood. They are either upbeat or morose, motivated or not, optimistic or pessimistic, involved or alienated. The team's ability to perform is determined by the emotional climate of the group. Do team members get along well? Do individuals feel valued and respected? Do they feel safe in the team? Do they respect each other? Team resonance is developed by establishing norms and practices that support the development of the four critical aspects of emotional intelligence: self-awareness, self-management, empathy, and positive relationships. When resonant individuals form a team, a culture is formed in which people feel safe to take the risks necessary to learn and work together toward their shared vision. Resonant leaders build resonant teams (Goleman, Boyatzis, & McKee, 2002).

Collins (2005) adds another layer of understanding to the complex concept of leadership. He differentiated between leadership and power, telling us that "true leadership only exists if people follow when they have the freedom not to" (p. 13). The reality of tenured faculty in schools means that there are potentially "a thousand points of no" for almost everything. School administrators must rely on their emotional intelligence as well as their ability to communicate effectively to illuminate people's inherent desire to do good work. They must work with staff to develop passion for a shared vision.

> School administrators must rely on their emotional intelligence as well as their ability to communicate effectively to illuminate people's inherent desire to do good work.

The five-level leadership hierarchy developed by Collins (2005) places effective leaders at Level 4 and describes them as able to "catalyze commitment to and vigorous pursuit of a clear and compelling vision, stimulating higher performance standards" (p. 12). Level 4 leaders are persuasive communicators and goal-setters. Level 5 leaders have a dual focus on performance and the development of leadership capacity in others. They differ from Level 4 leaders in that they are "ambitious first and foremost for the . . . vision—not themselves—and they have the will to do whatever it takes to make good on that ambition" (p. 11). Level 5 leaders bring to fruition the changes that are necessary to shift the school's culture to improve both student and staff achievement. This kind of leadership is about more than consensus-building and collaborating. It is about making sure that the "right decisions happen—no matter how difficult or painful" for sustained improvement of the school and the achievement of its vision—"independent of consensus or popularity" (p. 11). It is about doing whatever it takes to ensure learning for all!

In chapter 3, we talked about adaptive challenges and how changes in attitudes, habits, and even deeply held values are required to address them. We also talked about how confronting the need for major change generates conflict and resistance. Managing that conflict, dealing with the politics involved, and holding people accountable to agreed-upon values require that principals hold steady in the heat of action. Their job is to positively confront the conflict—to keep disequilibrium from getting out of hand and the conflict from becoming destructive. They must keep an unwavering focus on addressing the difficult issues with which they are dealing. Opting for a quick fix (that is, a program or strategy that looks good) might be tempting when the going gets rough; however, if deep sustainable change is to occur, the process must be seen through to its completion. In holding steady, administrators are likely to be the targets of considerable frustration and anger. This seems to go with the territory. Having well-developed emotional intelligence to draw upon in the process is critically important. Leadership for enduring change is not for the faint of heart!

▶ Leadership for enduring change is not for the faint of heart!

The Power of Culture

The goal in the school improvement process is to embed improved learning structures and strategies in the school's culture so that they become part of everyday practice. This work is full of twists and turns. It cannot be done without a solid understanding of and respect for the power of an organization's culture.

Simply stated, culture is "the way we do things around here." Schein (2004) defined it as the system of basic assumptions and beliefs that are accepted and ingrained—so much so that they are "automatically taught to new members . . . as the correct way to perceive, think and feel about problems" (p. 17). The culture of a group is affected by the length of time they have been together, membership stability, and the emotional intensity of the history they share. Based on shared learning experiences, basic assumptions develop and come to be taken for granted. Schein referred to core assumptions as critical genes in the cultural DNA of the group. They are reflected in the beliefs and norms espoused by the group. Teachers are typically the custodians of a school's culture because often they have been there for a number of years, whereas administrators tend to come and go.

School cultures are particularly ingrained and extremely difficult to change. Talking about culture, identifying elements of culture, and exploring the culture of other organizations will not precipitate change. What does give rise to change is a consensus that the old way of doing business does not align with a valued shared vision. When staff behavior shifts, the culture of a school shifts. It is our belief that the measure of a cultural shift is in the extent of the changes that are exhibited in staff behavior.

Peterson and Deal (2002) cautioned us to be very respectful when cultural shifts must occur. Good or bad, the existing culture of a group is understood by its members, and even the slightest change will throw it into disequilibrium. Rituals, traditions, and ceremonies are what Peterson and Deal called "culture in action." They suggested that highlighting a group's history is a way of recognizing and honoring its past. Storytelling is a powerful means of communicating important information about the group as well as reinforcing core values and purpose. The architecture, artifacts, and symbols associated with a group are visual cultural cues, tangible cultural touchstones that create stability. It is critical that efforts to change the culture be carefully thought out and implemented with full awareness that the changes will not go unnoticed.

> It is critical that efforts to change the culture be carefully thought out and implemented with full awareness that the changes will not go unnoticed.

Culture and Teacher Leadership

Schein (2004) noted that "culture creation and management are the essence of leadership," and that "leadership and culture are two sides of the same coin" (p. 1). Culture is created and must be managed as people work and live together. Strong leadership from those in formal positions is a necessary prerequisite to any school improvement efforts. It is also requisite for the creation of a culture that will support the development of teacher leadership.

Teacher leaders typically serve in either formal or informal leadership roles. Teacher leaders in formal roles are those who have titles such as department head, team leader, or lead teacher. People in these positions have typically applied for them and may have also received specialized training to assume responsibility for activities like facilitating workshops, implementing curricula, and managing department budgets. On the other hand, teachers in informal leadership roles have no "legitimate" (positional) authority.

Instead, their influence is a result of being recognized by their administrators and peers for their knowledge, skills, ability, and passion.

As with all leadership positions, the success or failure of teacher leaders is dependent upon their relationships with colleagues. That said, however, administrators must support informal teacher leaders in unique ways, given that they do not have the legitimate power afforded those in formal positions. Without careful planning to create a supportive school culture, those in informal leadership roles are likely to face daunting challenges. "The traditional norms of teaching—autonomy, egalitarianism and seniority—exert a powerful and persistent influence" that must be overcome (Johnson & Donaldson, 2007, p. 13). These norms can seriously undermine the efforts of teacher leaders to share their expertise and are a serious deterrent to the success of efforts to share leadership.

Danielson (2007) described an all-too-common scenario in which those who stick their heads up risk being cut down to size. In Australia, this is called the "tall poppy syndrome." It is what happens when administrators or teachers stand in the way of those who are willing to take on leadership roles.

It falls to the principal to be proactive in shifting the school's culture to support shared leadership by establishing and reinforcing a new set of norms that promote collegial and collaborative working relationships, breaking down classroom or department boundaries, and acknowledging expertise. This can be done by clearly defining informal teacher leadership roles. What roles will be established? What responsibilities will the role encompass? What qualifications must the person filling the role have? The school administration needs to explain the teacher leadership plan carefully to the entire staff to clarify the purpose for it and the process that will be followed in selecting people to assume the identified roles. It must be clear that teacher leaders are not viewed as extra help for administrators; rather, their purpose is to work with their colleagues to improve student achievement and school success. Instructional leadership must be their priority.

> ▶ It must be clear that teacher leaders are not viewed as extra help for administrators.

Administrators can take tangible steps to make informal teacher leadership a viable part of the school's culture through providing common planning and release time to work with colleagues. Those in teacher leader roles can be given further credibility and support through specialized training in topics such as group facilitation, the use of data to inform practice, curriculum planning, assessment design, and differentiated instruction. Training in the skills of consulting and coaching is also important for teachers in these roles.

Through fostering an environment in which it is safe for teachers to express ideas and take professional risks, administrators can promote the collaborative working relationships that are necessary for informal teacher leadership to flourish. In such an environment, the tall poppy syndrome is noticeably absent. The success of teacher leadership roles is dependent upon proactive, ongoing, tangible support from the school's administration.

The Power of Shared Leadership in Navigating the Change Process

Fullan (2001) described change as disturbing the system and cautioned that there is a time to disturb and a time to cohere. Effective leaders understand that chaos and feelings of disorientation are natural when change efforts are underway. They strive to engage people with different points of view and do not shy away from the conflict that is likely to result. In fact, they recognize the potential for creativity and innovation that is inherent in chaos. Shared leadership has the potential to have a powerful impact on the change process. The more people share leadership responsibilities, the greater the chance to move the change process forward, while at the same time being cognizant of its impact on the school as a whole. Teacher leaders can influence the process by sharing their unique perspectives and assisting with the planning.

> ▶ Teacher leaders can influence the change process by sharing their unique perspectives and assisting with the planning.

As staff members engage in new learning and new practice, it is important to recognize progress early in the process. Quick wins that can be touted and celebrated will encourage and support new learning. In order to keep the momentum alive, it is necessary to keep a watchful eye on energy levels, because it is "energy, not time" that is the "fundamental currency of high performance" (Fullan, 2005, p. 26). Sustained periods of intensity and new learning wear people out. They become weary as a result of feeling constantly challenged and pushed. The work loses its excitement, passion flags, and the culture is at risk of becoming negative and debilitating. Effective leaders work to restore energy by easing off for periods of time to allow learning to be consolidated. Recognition for progress and celebrations of achievement are critically important to the energy replenishment process.

Key Cultural Shifts to Improve School and Student Success

Teacher leaders can play an integral role in the school improvement process. There are nine key cultural shifts that can be made that will ensure improved student achievement and school success. Teacher leaders can play a critical role in facilitating these shifts. The key cultural shifts are as follows:

1. **From an emphasis on teaching to an emphasis on learning.** Emphasis on content coverage is replaced with emphasis on demonstration of student proficiency. Teachers as well as students are learners.

2. **From teacher isolation to collaboration.** Teachers' roles shift from being the authority in their own classrooms to becoming members of a team of learners. Teacher independence is replaced with interdependence.

3. **From having a pass/fail mindset to eliminating failure.** Student success is ensured by providing adequate time and opportunity to learn. Students no longer have only one chance to pass (win) or fail (lose).

4. **From compliance to commitment.** Teachers move from doing what they are expected to do (doing a job) to demonstrating passion for and excitement about the difference they are making for students.

5. **From curriculum overload to a guaranteed curriculum.** The "covering the curriculum" mindset is replaced with identification of essential outcomes that can be covered in the time available.

6. **From being busy to getting results.** Teachers are and will always be busy; however, when the focus shifts from being busy to getting results, teachers view their role in the learning process differently. With this shift, learning for all is indeed possible.

7. **From schoolwide goals to team goals.** While goals that impact the entire school continue to be important, teachers also work in smaller, specialized teams to set goals that affect student achievement at specific levels in specific areas.

8. **From static assessment to dynamic assessment.** Assessment *of* learning or evaluation of student proficiency (static assessment) is enhanced by assessment *for* and *as* learning (dynamic assessment)

that focuses on demonstration of student proficiency. Assessment *for* and *as* learning is dynamic and involves students in their own learning. At the same time, it gives teachers the information they need to appropriately plan instruction. Although static and dynamic assessments have different purposes, they are both valuable.

9. **From over-the-wall to flexible organization.** The lock-step progression of students from year to year is replaced with flexibility that allows students sufficient time on task and opportunity to learn in the areas that cause them to struggle before they are given new material.

What the Lesson Teaches Us

- Leadership is about influencing others to move in a common direction.

- Leadership is an improvisational activity requiring many varied skills and perspectives.

- Strong relationships and the ability to communicate honestly are critical.

- A strong, clearly articulated vision is the prerequisite for effective leadership.

- Emotional intelligence is a key ingredient to building the team resonance required by a successful learning community.

- The culture of an organization is powerful and must be understood.

- Efforts to change culture must be undertaken thoughtfully and with respect.

- There is a time to disturb (orchestrate change) and a time to cohere (regroup and re-energize).

- There is seldom a convenient time or sufficient buy-in from staff to begin the improvement process.

- Often buy-in comes as a result of experiencing the change process.

- Resistance can take many forms and wreak havoc on change efforts. Resistors must not be allowed to frustrate the efforts of those who are eager to move forward. Leaders must stay the course and avoid being sidetracked.

- The job of school administrators is too huge and complex to be managed by only those in formal leadership positions.

- Leadership must be shared or distributed to be effective.

- Teacher leaders will flounder without deliberate, tangible support from administrators.

- Supportive cultural norms, structures, resources, and incentives must be established to ensure the success of teacher leadership efforts.

- There are some leadership issues that reside solely in the administrative domain.

- Leadership that results in a sustained culture shift is not for sissies.

Lessons Lived: A Story From the Real World

Strong leadership predicated on solid character and tenacity is the key ingredient for change that results in lasting school improvement. Leadership must be informed by an understanding of and respect for the power of organizational culture if change initiatives are to be successfully implemented and sustained.

Pierre Elliott Trudeau Elementary School

In May 2000, Marian Lothian became the principal of Pierre Elliott Trudeau Elementary School, a K–6 school in Gatineau, Quebec. At that time, the school was known as Pius XII Elementary School. Two years earlier, the province had passed a law abolishing all Quebec confessional schools and forming new linguistic schools. Catholic and Protestant schools were organized according to language of instruction.

Pius XII Elementary School had been an English Catholic school in a predominantly French Catholic system. The school, situated next door to a Catholic church, had a long history in the community. It prided itself on providing a solid education to inner-city children. Prior to the restructuring, the population of the school had been steadily declining. With the introduction of students from the former English Protestant school system, however, the population doubled.

The student population is very diverse with many learning challenges. There is a high aboriginal population for whom Cree is the first language. In recent years, the school population has grown significantly and has become increasingly multicultural. With that change in population has come a higher ELL population (30%) and a need to support cultural diversity in positive ways. The percentage of the student population with special education needs is also 30%.

When Marian arrived, 2 years had gone by since the restructuring, and nothing had visibly changed in the school. The two school communities (Catholic and Protestant) that had been amalgamated were sharing the same building, but little else. Protestant parents were unhappy about the forced change, and Catholic parents fiercely held on to their traditions. Crosses still adorned the walls and halls, as did a picture of Pope Pius XII. The school's interior was dark and decrepit, in need of refurbishment. English instruction was located on the first floor and French Immersion on the second floor. Only English was spoken on the first floor and only French on the second floor. Although they followed the same Quebec curriculum and taught students at the same level and age, staff in the English and French programs did not work together.

Because it was an English school in a predominantly French system, there were very few instructional resources. Those that did exist were outdated. In addition, the professional growth opportunities offered to the English Catholic educators had been limited. The Protestant educators, on the other hand, had a completely different background. They were equipped with many resources and embraced ongoing professional development. There were marked cultural differences between the two groups, and neither group was particularly pleased about their circumstances.

Marian had a clear mandate and support for change from the district's director-general and the board. The parent community was also supportive of change and, in fact, expected it. Nevertheless, Marian viewed her new position with trepidation and knew that she would have to take some risks to kick-start the reculturing process that was so desperately needed. She knew that whatever she did would have to touch all staff members; otherwise, she feared that they would simply continue to do things the way they always had. So much change was needed on so many levels that she worried that she would not be able to build a team with the staff and that she might forever be viewed as "the enemy to be endured." Marian knew going in that she would need a thick skin. Little did she know just how thick it would have to be!

A Year to Remember

Marian realized that there was much work to be done where both student and staff learning was concerned. She committed to begin addressing those issues immediately upon her arrival at the school. She would give priority to curricular alignment, instructional practice, and the acquisition of appropriate resources to support learning. She committed to doing whatever it took to facilitate teacher collaboration and professional growth. When Marian arrived at the school, the Quebec Education Plan (QEP) was just beginning to be implemented, and she seized the opportunity to use it as a tool for the work she had to do.

The QEP, the provincial plan for school reform, demands sweeping educational change. In the QEP, grades have been replaced by 2-year cycles in which educational competencies have been identified for each level of the cycle as well as end-of-cycle testing. It is a constructivist approach that focuses on student learning in the social context. School principals are charged with the responsibility for implementing the plan and facilitating the professional development that is inherent in it.

Marian realized that she would have to back any changes she initiated with a clearly articulated vision, complete with sound rationale and well-thought-out strategy. She had decided that her debut as the principal needed to be broad and significant. So, she took the plunge by announcing that the school would be reorganized so that classes would be arranged by cycles rather than by language of instruction. This change would allow teachers to collaborate on themes and joint projects as envisioned by the QEP.

Many staff members responded by informing her that they did *not* want this change and that she would have to understand that they were accustomed to making the decisions in the school. Marian replied that she took her role as principal very seriously; the staff would have to understand that the decision had been made. She went on to say that what was needed now was their input as to how this change would take place. She provided the staff with blueprints of the school and delivered a visionary speech about how, eventually, they would become a Lead school in the QEP. For now, however, they would start with restructuring their school to be in line with the QEP philosophy. The only criterion she placed on the staff's deliberations was that classes had to be arranged in proximity by cycles. About 10 days later, she received the staff plan, along with a note saying they still didn't want to change classes around. Marian purposely made no changes to the plan; instead, she sent a note thanking them for their insightful work. She told them they could immediately start to rearrange their classes according to their plan. Then she rolled up her sleeves and helped them make the move. In Marian's words, "My debut as principal certainly did not go unnoticed, but nor did it receive a thunderous applause from the teachers for an encore. Our parents watched from the sidelines."

Two other very sensitive changes were made during Marian's first year at the school that made it a year to remember: removing the crosses and changing the name of the school to a less Catholic name.

When school opened in the fall, teachers were informed that because they were now a nondenominational school, the crosses would have to be taken down. This move had significant repercussions. Some perceived Marian as challenging the core of the school's history and culture. While she told staff members that she would find appropriate homes for the crosses, many could not be appeased. In fact, some openly declared that they would not take them down. Marian told them she understood that this was difficult and that she would arrange to have the maintenance staff remove them at a later date. During the year, all of the crosses found their way into Marian's office, and the staff was watching—wondering what she was going to do with them. What she did was offer a cross to anyone who would like one. Requests from the staff were given priority. The local priest was invited to offer crosses to his parishioners as well. By the end of the year, more people wanted crosses than there were crosses to give. In preparation for distributing them, Marian personally polished each cross and then had it mounted with a brass plaque that had been engraved with the name of the school, the year, and the name of the person receiving it. Marian made personal calls to each person who did not receive one.

Perhaps the most acrimonious first-year activity of all surrounded changing the name of the school to name it after former Prime Minister Pierre Elliott Trudeau, at the time of his death in September 2000. This initiative was largely undertaken by the parent community (mostly former Protestant parents). Because other schools in the area were also vying for the opportunity to use his name, it was necessary to move quickly. Despite Marian's best efforts to explain the process involved in renaming the school and to invite staff input, many refused to engage. They blamed her for the change and directed considerable rancor toward her. Several months of tension followed. While it was a very difficult time, Marian had opportunities to address issues like honesty, integrity, team membership, and shared responsibility. When many of the staff would not talk with their students about the name change, Marian herself visited classes to speak with them about the reason for the new school name and how it had been chosen. She got students involved in selecting the new school colors and had competitions to design new school crests. Over time, Marian's commitment and modeling won the day. By June of that year, when the official renaming ceremony was held, staff morale had turned around. They had become involved and supportive. As part of the ceremony, the crosses were given to their new owners and a memorabilia wall was unveiled. On it was placed a cross that had been mounted in a shadow box, a picture of Pope Pius XII, and photographs of years gone by. The parish priest attended to bless the school and the new name. It was a dignified ceremony attended by many special guests and the press.

Throughout that year, and in the years that followed, Marian consciously attempted to temper her strong approach with what she calls "a selective good dose of caring and supportive leadership." She actively supported teachers by writing thank-you notes for any signs of support and often included little treats with the notes. She gave teachers plants on the first day of school and handed out apples in the fall as a means of saying thank you for getting the year off to a good start. She also hosted wine and cheese gatherings and generally watched for ways to offer the staff recognition and appreciation.

Over the course of that dramatic first year, teachers came to accept that the school was moving ahead to forge a new future; and while they did not always appreciate Marian's leadership or agree with the changes, none resigned or requested a transfer. The stage had been set for other changes to take place.

Creating a Culture of Learning

Using the QEP as a tool to guide the work, Marian made the creation of a culture of learning a priority from the first year. Through conversation with the staff, she was able to determine that literacy was an area in which they were interested. She saw this as a positive hook and latched onto it as a means of getting started. Marian recognized that as a first-time elementary school principal, she had a lot of personal professional learning to do to become equipped to guide teachers in the literacy area. With guidance from the provincial support team, Marian became immersed in literacy teaching practice and soon discovered both a vision and a model for literacy teaching that would guide her work with teachers. She acquired the knowledge, under-standing, and confidence she needed to move forward with the school's literacy initiative. She had also modeled an acceptance of the need to continu-ally learn and grow professionally.

Marian focused on student assessment and reporting, as well as the implementation of the QEP, as a means of advancing the literacy initiative. She knew that she needed an assessment tool that would provide an impe-tus for teachers to alter their practices. With that in mind, Marian formed a team of teachers and a parent from the school's Governing Board. Their mandate was to create a new student report card based on QEP standards. The team reviewed reports from other schools and ultimately developed a new report card for their school. The power in this strategy arose from the fact that as teachers began to use the new report card, they quickly real-ized that to accurately evaluate the different competencies across the sub-ject domains, they needed to teach and assess differently. Marian responded by facilitating professional development in areas the teachers identified as needing attention. From that point on, planning for professional develop-ment was a shared, collaboratively planned activity.

The work done on the report card served as a catalyst to shift the school's learning culture. While the work on assessment and effective reporting origi-nated with the school's focus on literacy, the reality is that it, along with the professional development that followed, had a pervasive impact on all areas of the school.

Looking Back With Satisfaction

Over 7 years, though the culture of Pierre Elliott Trudeau Elementary School shifted significantly on many different levels, the emphasis was always on learning—for staff and students. Gone are the workbooks and practice of teachers working in isolation. Today, dialogue and collaboration about teach-ing and learning are the norm. Teacher teams routinely work together to plan instruction, use assessment to improve student achievement, and search for ways to assist struggling students. Professional development is rich and diverse. True to Marian's prediction, Pierre Elliott Trudeau Elementary has become a Lead school in the Quebec Education Plan. The teachers from Trudeau Elementary are recognized provincially for their work in assess-ment and reporting. They are often invited to share what they learned with other teachers. They have piloted various assessment initiatives and are cur-rently working on a major grant from the province to research how student portfolios and student-led conferencing can replace a traditional report card, in accordance with changes made to the Quebec Education Act. Although the student population presents numerous challenges with high numbers of special education and ELL students, literacy results since 2002 have improved. The staff of Pierre Elliott Trudeau Elementary School functions as a learning community. Leadership is shared, and all teachers accept responsibility for keeping the school's learning culture rich and vibrant.

As the culture shifted, Marian realized that she had "slowly moved from change agent to educational leader—with a deeper sense of pedagogy now driving our professional learning community." She had become a leader of leaders. The necessary cultural changes had been made so that she was able to share the leadership in the school and turn her attention to learning and student achievement. In reflecting on her work with the staff, Marian says, "I have come to the realization that although there are key elements that bonded to create an environment in which teaching practices shifted, it really is a sum total of all the little things that, by themselves, at the time seemed small and unimportant to the big picture that were critical to the formation of the essential components of trust, informed risk-taking, and professionalism that changed practices."

Pierre Elliott Trudeau Elementary School has been and continues to be on a journey of continuous improvement that is neither linear nor predictable. Throughout the journey, Marian has pushed the staff to grow professionally, while at the same time modeling personal commitment to professional growth through pursuing her doctoral degree. In her words, "What legacy I will leave this school when all is said and done, I hope, will be professional pride on the part of the teaching staff that will carry them to always strive to be the best they can be as teachers, not to fear new ideas and changes to teaching practices, and to continue growing professionally." Over the course of her time there, a community of instructional leaders was formed.

Marian became assistant director of educational services with the Western Quebec School Board in October 2007. It is safe to say that Marian's legacy will live on and that the staff will continue to learn and grow professionally as a result of her leadership.

Summary

The reality of leadership that results in significant reculturing and school improvement is that there is no easy way to do it. There is never a convenient time, nor are there recipes that will guarantee success. There is always risk involved, and people will seldom embrace the prospect of change. In fact, staff buy-in usually comes after the change process is already underway. Teachers want to be successful—to make a difference in the lives of their students—and sometimes a principal needs to take a strong stand to precipitate the work that will result in the improved practice that will allow that to happen.

A strong, clearly articulated vision is necessary for any reculturing effort. It provides the foundation and filter for the day-to-day nitty-gritty work that must be done to enact the changes that will make a difference to learning for both students and teachers. When leadership is distributed throughout the staff, the process is enhanced, and the likelihood of it being sustained is greater.

Chapter 5 deals with the importance of measurement, the third lesson learned from successful schools.

Measurement Matters . . .
But Not to Everyone

In *Harbors of Hope,* we made a distinction between *planning to plan* and *planning to improve.* Schools that plan to plan spend time and energy searching for innovative programs, materials, and procedures to implement. While planning-to-plan intentions are honorable, this approach lacks direction and strategy. It is an approach that capitalizes on good ideas rather than on good planning. A plan to improve, on the other hand, is based on the examination of meaningful data and the establishment of clear goals that, when achieved, will provide evidence that improvement has occurred. Change and improvement are impossible to track and validate without using data as a guide. The collection of baseline data provides the starting point. Subsequent measurements can then be compared with the baseline to evaluate progress toward goals.

> Change and improvement are impossible to track and validate without using data as a guide.

As you have seen in previous chapters, changing practice is really about changing a school's culture, and that can be very difficult. The need to make measurement a priority may not be readily understood and accepted. Until they realize the power inherent in using critical evidence to guide planning, some teachers may view the gathering of data negatively and with suspicion, fearing that it may be used to evaluate their performance. Others may be leery of gathering data because they do not know how to use it effectively. Still others may resist because they are reluctant to embrace the new learning and the changed behavior it requires. Until educators become comfortable with analyzing and using data, they may have difficulty seeing why it is such an integral part of the planning process. Strong leadership that supports the development of teacher assessment literacy and pedagogical capacity is required to embed and sustain effective measurement practices in the school's culture.

The Link to Effective Schools Research

The prominent correlate found in the lesson for this chapter is "frequent monitoring of student progress." In pursuing the effective schools mission of "learning for all—whatever it takes," we must gather performance data that tell us who is learning and who is not, and then use it to adjust instruction accordingly. Lezotte and McKee (2002) noted that schools "must be explicit and intentional about what they plan to measure and monitor" to gauge the extent to which the 'learning for all' mission is being accomplished" (p. 145). They recommended three rules of thumb to guide measurement practice:

1. Strike a balance between too much and too little data.

2. Choose data sources that can be monitored over time.

3. Choose data that is aligned with clearly identified essential learner outcomes. (p. 146)

Lezotte and McKee also pointed out the importance of making data user-friendly or readily accessible to those who will be using it. To be *user-friendly,* data must be disaggregated in meaningful ways to allow staff to clearly see where they are currently, set relevant goals, and monitor progress toward them. When schools use frequent monitoring to help all students achieve success with essential outcomes, they have made the transition from "teaching-centered organizations to proactive, learner-centered educational communities" (Lezotte & McKee, 2002, p. 19).

> In schools that are Harbors of Hope, learning by all is a reality. In these schools, the correlates work in concert and are interdependent. All seven are consistently present and powerfully demonstrated.

What We Have Learned About the Lesson

Schools are inundated with many different kinds of data from many different sources. Different data are important to different stakeholders. The challenge in planning to improve is to find the data that provide *critical evidence* for the people using it. For example, data that are critical evidence for administrators may hold little meaning for classroom teachers. By the same token, what is critical evidence for classroom teachers may not give administrators the information they require. Planning to improve revolves around collecting, organizing, and analyzing the evidence (data) that is critical to those who will use it. When schools have determined what they value, they will know which measurements provide critical evidence for tracking school and student success. Only when data are analyzed within the values framework can they become meaningful. Until then, measurement results are just numbers.

▶ The challenge in planning to improve is to find the data that provide *critical evidence* for the people using it.

Measurement in this era of accountability goes far beyond surface considerations of student achievement to include all aspects of both student and teacher learning. In the words of Douglas Reeves (2006), "Accountability includes the actions of adults, not merely the scores of students" (p. 83). It necessitates that educators reflect on every facet of their teaching practice. Do we know our students' achievement levels? Do we understand our students' learning needs? Are we meeting the needs of all students? Are our interventions timely and effective? Do students have full opportunity and adequate time to learn? Are our curricula aligned? Have we determined which learning outcomes are essential? Are we assessing what we teach? Are we using assessment information to inform our practice? Are school policies and practices effective and fully understood? Have we allocated resources appropriately? Combining values-based critical evidence with a solid planning process provides a framework within which to explore the answers to these questions.

A School Improvement Analogy

School improvement planning can be compared with airline travel. The priority of airline pilots and crew is the safety and comfort of passengers. They are supported by ground crew and air-traffic controllers.

Prior to take off, the maintenance crew examines the plane, calibrates the gauges, and checks them for accuracy according to the plane's critical functions. The pilot files a flight plan. Among other things, the flight plan cites the final destination, the route to be taken, the altitude at which the plane will fly, and the estimated time of arrival. Once airborne, the pilot and copilot focus on flying the plane, while the cabin crew focuses on the safety and comfort of the passengers. All crew members routinely use both qualitative and quantitative data to do their work. When new procedures or technologies become available, they take the required training in order to be as effective as possible in their positions.

The pilot and copilot keep a close eye on the gauges in the cockpit because they provide critical evidence for the flight. They know what the baseline readings are, and they know which readings constitute normal progress and which ones do not. They recognize when the readings indicate that a change or in-flight correction is required, and they make the necessary adjustments to fix whatever is interfering with the plane's progress toward its destination. The cabin crew knows how many people are on board, where they are situated, and whether any passengers might require special attention during the flight. They have the expertise to deal with emergency situations if necessary, and their focus is on reading the environment in the cabin. Are the passengers aware of and following safety procedures? Are the passengers comfortable? Is anyone in distress? Does anyone need anything? Working as a team that shares common values and goals, the people responsible for the flight, both in the air and on the ground, do what is required to ensure that the final destination is reached safely.

Schools that plan to improve follow a process similar to an airline flight. The destination is success for all students, and the flight plan is the clearly articulated school improvement plan. Many people are involved in the process, and their work is guided by shared values and common goals. Based on their values, the staff collect critical evidence that provides baseline information about such things as student achievement, curriculum alignment, assessment practices, the learning climate, deportment, and safety issues. This is the educational equivalent of calibrating the gauges in preparation for a flight. Strengths and limitations are identified, goals for improvement are set, and a school plan is developed. Through this process, educators file their "flight plan." As work proceeds, measurements are taken on a regular basis to assess progress toward goals. When it appears that the expected progress is not being made, plans are reviewed and adjusted accordingly to get things on track for success. Working as a team, staff members do what is required to achieve the goals that have been set—to reach the destination that has been chosen. Sometimes that means making changes on the fly. While airline crews use physical and technical information to reach their destinations, successful schools use measurement, staff learning, and professional development. Teachers are seen as learners, and continuous professional development is an accepted responsibility.

Schools that plan to improve follow a planning process similar to the one used to plan an airline flight. The destination is success for all students, and the flight plan is the clearly articulated school improvement plan.

Ongoing gathering, analyzing, and responding to data or critical evidence are basic to successful flights and successful school planning. Both qualitative and quantitative measurements provide needed critical evidence. The following sections summarize some of the critical considerations that are central to developing a data-driven plan to improve.

Measurement Matters: Gauging Perceptions

Qualitative measures identify perceptions, attitudes, and opinions. Perceptions are linked to attitudes and opinions, and they strongly influence how information is interpreted and acted upon. For most people, perceptions are their reality. Anne Conzemius and Jan O'Neill (2002) indicated that "understanding perceptions is key to identifying areas of satisfaction and opportunities for improvement" (p. 115). They identified three commonly used techniques for gathering perceptual data: in-depth interviews, focus groups, and surveys. The following guidelines (Conzemius & O'Neill, 2002) are important for collecting perceptual data:

- It is important to gather data from a representative sample (a microcosm) of the larger community.

- Stratification or gathering data from various subgroups is also important.

- Disaggregating or dividing results from various subgroups helps with analysis.

- It is important to develop easily understood questions to get easily analyzed data. Questions can be either open-ended or closed, depending upon the information being sought.

- Scales can be used to quantify some data (such as how many people agree with certain statements).

Measurement Matters: Tracking Student Performance

Measuring student performance is a complex and multifaceted issue because there are many kinds of measurement options employed by different stakeholders. Information about student achievement has different value depending upon the perspective of the people analyzing it. *External assessment programs* typically take the form of standardized tests. They serve a purpose divisionally, provincially, and nationally. *Internal assessment programs* are classroom-based and provide teachers with the information they need to plan and implement appropriate instruction. The key to constructive use of critical evidence is to celebrate the good news that is found in it and confront the brutal facts with a determination to problem-solve and make improvements.

> The key to constructive use of critical evidence is to celebrate the good news that is found in it and confront the brutal facts with a determination to problem-solve and make improvements.

External Assessment Programs

Standardized tests are broad-scale external assessments developed to measure student progress on provincial or national standards. They may be either criterion- or norm-referenced and are typically administered under uniform conditions. They sample student achievement in certain disciplines or skill areas. The results are used to ascertain the success of curriculum implementation throughout the province. Because the tests are administered annually, they provide useful longitudinal data. This information is useful for analyzing patterns of achievement over time and planning to overcome deficits. Results of standardized tests provide a big-picture look at how groups of students are performing within their local population and compared to other schools or divisions. They can be disaggregated according to criteria such as program, gender, or ethnicity to determine how one subgroup is achieving relative to other subgroups.

At the school level, teachers and administrators can analyze results to determine overall achievement on standards in their school. The information can be used to guide school improvement planning. Viewed from a central office perspective, individual school results are useful for divisional planning. Provincially, division results provide information for looking ahead.

Standardized testing does not effectively influence classroom practice. The tests have limited use in terms of providing classroom teachers with information that could assist them with planning instruction to meet individual student needs. They are not useful for identifying students at risk or underachieving students, and they do not provide information about learning styles and attitudes. In view of the fact that standardized tests are not administered at all grade levels, there are gaps in the information they provide. Often, the delay between students being tested and teachers receiving the results is significant. In fact, results from tests administered in the spring are typically not released until fall. By then, teachers and students are already into a new school year. There are other, more effective ways of gathering information about individual students that can be used to inform instruction.

Internal/Classroom Assessment Programs

There are three distinct but related purposes for classroom assessment: assessment *for* learning, assessment *as* learning, and assessment *of* learning. All serve different but equally valuable purposes.

Assessment *for* learning provides teachers with a starting point (baseline information) on each student's current level of skill or knowledge and uses periodic subsequent assessment to monitor student growth. It is both formative and diagnostic, providing information about student readiness to learn. Assessment *for* learning can also be called *preassessment*. In addition to yielding information about current skill levels, it also provides insight about student learning styles, multiple intelligences, attitudes toward learning, and students' perceptions of themselves as learners. Assessment *for* learning informs instruction by providing teachers with the information they need to differentiate teaching and learning activities to meet individual learning needs. It is useful for targeting instruction and learning resources, as well as for providing students with feedback that will help them grow.

Assessment *as* learning focuses on the development of metacognition in students. *Metacognition* is learning about learning. Students with a well-developed metacognitive sense understand how they learn and know how to go about it. They know how to tap into their prior knowledge to make sense of information and use it for new understanding. They can analyze, reflect on, and monitor their own learning to acquire new skills and arrive at new insights. Effective instruction supports students in the acquisition of metacognitive skills and attitudes.

Assessment *of* learning is used to confirm what students know and can do, as well as to demonstrate student proficiency on curricular outcomes. It is summative in nature—a snapshot of where students are at a point in time. Results gathered from assessment *of* learning activities are used for reporting purposes and for setting goals for future progress.

Assessment *for* learning provides starting points for instruction and information about student progress as they learn.

Assessment *as* learning develops student metacognition.

Assessment *of* learning confirms what students know and can do at a point in time.

In an effective assessment program, student involvement is a priority. The assessment practices are balanced and well-designed, consisting of multiple measurement strategies that take into account student learning styles and needs, and provide critical evidence for reporting purposes. Rick Stiggins and his coauthors (2004) offered five keys to accurate classroom assessment that is used effectively:

1. **Clear purposes.** How assessment is constructed and used depends upon its purpose. It is critical to know why assessment is being done. If its purpose is to enhance learning, students should understand that it is their opportunity to demonstrate what they know and can do without worrying about grades being assigned. If its purpose is to check proficiency on learning outcomes, students must be aware that they will be graded. As well, teachers need to ensure that the assessment is of excellent quality because of its potential impact on students and the school.

2. **Clear targets.** Teachers must determine which learning targets are being assessed in order to ensure that the assessment is accurate and the results are useful. The targets must be clearly stated and interpreted for students in friendly language so that they understand what they are being assessed on. Rubrics and scoring guides provide additional information to help students understand what is being asked of them.

3. **Good design.** A well-designed assessment program uses a variety of assessment tools to measure the complete range of thinking and learning. It gives students the chance to demonstrate their proficiency in many different ways. Just as effective instruction is differentiated to address student learning needs, effective assessment is also differentiated. Differentiated assessment practice ensures that students will have multiple opportunities to show or demonstrate what they know and can do. Sometimes the most effective way to assess is by using traditional measures such as fill in the blank,

true/false, multiple choice, labeling diagrams, drawing graphs, and so on. At other times, the most effective measures involve performance assessments in which students demonstrate their proficiency through writing essays, doing projects, journaling, compiling a portfolio, displaying art work, doing a play, singing, or playing an instrument, and so on. Good assessment design identifies which assessments are for formative purposes and which are for grading purposes. It also ensures that students are adequately supported in order to avoid bias. Bias is anything that interferes with a student's ability to demonstrate proficiency and applies to students for whom English is the second language as well as those with interfering emotional or physical conditions.

4. **Sound communication.** Effective assessment practice ensures that all concerned know which measurements are for formative purposes and which are for evaluation. How will information be stored and managed? How and when will reporting be done? Which assessments are for external reporting purposes? Which are for internal reporting? Which are for student information alone? How will students be involved in the reporting process?

5. **Student involvement.** A good assessment program will ensure that students understand learning targets and are involved in tracking their own progress. They will learn how to reflect on and communicate about their learning. Goal setting will be an integral part of their daily work. Portfolios and student-involved conferences are ideal ways to develop student skill in these areas.

Reeves (2006) touted the use of frequent common assessments and constructive use of the data they yield. He contended that "successful schools do not give a second thought to decisive and immediate interventions, including changing schedules, providing double classes for literacy and math, requiring homework supervision, breaking down major projects into incremental steps and otherwise providing preventive assistance for students in need" (p. 87).

▶ Common assessments, used effectively, are integral to aligning instruction and making intervention decisions when students are struggling.

Fullan, Hill, and Crevola (2006) underlined the benefits of effective measurement practice in their "breakthrough" model. They suggested that we must move away from what has always been done toward a new reality that ultimately "puts students in control of their learning process" (p. 11). They speak of the "Triple P Core Components" in their breakthrough system: personalization, precision, and professional learning, all of which are guided by shared moral purpose.

Triple P Model for Educational Breakthrough

- **Personalization:** Individualized instruction for all students according to their learning needs

- **Precision:** Planning instruction based on formative "pre-test" information and ongoing monitoring as learning progresses

- **Professional Learning:** Teacher growth in ability to identify essential outcomes and use formative assessment to plan instruction and respond to student learning needs

(Fullan, Hill, & Crevola, 2006)

Personalization refers to ensuring that each student receives instruction that supports his or her unique learning and motivational needs on an ongoing basis. It is, essentially, individualized instruction. *Precision* is about using data to plan instruction. It involves pretesting to ascertain starting points for instruction, post-testing to ensure that students have reached the targets before moving on to new learning, and early intervention when students are struggling. Student profiles that summarize each student's measurement results on identified outcomes are developed. Profiles are regularly updated as new measurement results are gathered. Precision instruction supports Royce Sadler's (1989) assertion that students should be able to answer three basic questions as they learn: What am I learning? Where am I now? What do I need to do to close the gap? The key to supporting student learning is critical evidence, gathered from measurement that is accurate and effectively used.

In order to personalize instruction, precision is required. Precision demands focused, ongoing *professional learning* for all teachers. When teacher learning is job-embedded or contextual, it is instruction- and student-specific. Curricula can be mapped, learning objectives and outcomes identified, methods of measuring and monitoring progress developed, and structures for intervention and assistance created. As teachers learn together, optimal school and classroom organization can be developed and home/school partnerships nurtured. Working in professional learning communities, teachers create knowledge about instruction through discussion and shared research.

As discussed in chapter 4, effective leadership that is distributed throughout the staff is critical to every aspect of school improvement. Where the accurate and effective use of measurement is concerned, the leadership role is to provide purpose and professional support for all teachers to collect and use the critical evidence they need in order to maximize instructional practice and student learning.

Six Core Functions to Support the Triple P Model

1. Assessment literacy

2. School and classroom organization

3. Classroom teaching

4. Professional learning communities

5. Intervention and assistance

6. Home and school/community partnerships

(Fullan, Hill, & Crevola, 2006, p. 91)

What the Lesson Teaches Us

- As Albert Einstein once noted, everything that can be counted isn't worth counting, and everything that is worth counting isn't always countable.

- Data are abundant in schools.

- Shared values and purpose identify which data are important.

- Important data are critical evidence and should be used to guide planning for school and student success.

- Critical evidence may be qualitative or quantitative.

- Qualitative data give information about perceptions, attitudes, and opinions.

- Quantitative data give numerical information that can be used to analyze, plan, and predict.

- Measurement processes may be external or internal. The purposes for each vary.

- Measurement results have different levels of relevance depending upon the roles of the people analyzing them.

- Measurement is as much about curriculum implementation and instructional practice as it is about student achievement.

- Used effectively, measurement results lead to the examination of curricular outcomes, curriculum alignment, assessment practices, instructional planning, and intervention strategies for struggling students.

- The effective use of measurement data requires that teachers adopt a learning stance in order to know their students and plan for optimal instruction.

- Classroom assessment focuses on assessment *for, as,* and *of* learning.

- The purposes for assessment must be understood, and the targets being assessed must be clearly articulated.

- Effective classroom assessment practice is differentiated to allow students to show what they know and can do in a variety of ways.

- Students benefit from reflection on their own learning and involvement in the assessment process.

- It is important to gather baseline or starting point data on students and to assess periodically as instruction unfolds in order to both measure progress and intervene with students who are struggling as soon as their difficulties are evident.

- Teachers collaborating on curriculum, assessment, and student achievement create knowledge together to improve practice.

- Strong shared leadership is critically important to the collection of pertinent data.

Lesson Lived: Stories From the Real World

The three stories that follow illustrate the power of using data or critical evidence to guide school improvement efforts. The stories featured here are illustrative of effective measurement at all levels in the school system.

Holy Trinity Catholic High School

John Burroughs is in his fourth year as principal of Holy Trinity Catholic High School. He declares that "no kid is invisible" in his school. Since Holy Trinity has a population of 1,179 students from grades 9–12, this is a substantial claim. We were interested to learn how John and the staff ensure that none of their students are invisible.

Holy Trinity opened in 2002 in Simcoe, Ontario, which is situated in an agricultural area. Most of the student population enjoys a comfortable middle-class lifestyle derived from farming. The population is relatively stable, and transience does not pose a big problem for the school. Grade-level populations are as follows: Grade 9 has 280 students; grade 10 has 275 students; grade 11 has 280 students; and grade 12 has 344 students. There are 74 fulltime equivalent classroom teachers.

Holy Trinity offers a full range of programs, from locally developed (LD) basic life and job skills to workplace, applied, and academic courses. Included in the range of programs are construction, transportation, manufacturing, foods/hospitality, hairstyling/cosmetology, information and communication technology (ICT), and computer engineering. A technologically advanced school with up-to-date equipment and processes, Holy Trinity is also a designated Cisco Networking Academy, which means they can provide online courses, interactive tools, and lab activities to help students develop the skills needed to fill information and communication technology positions in virtually every type of industry. Students at Holy Trinity have the opportunity to prepare for a variety of postsecondary pathways, such as apprenticeship, college or university entrance, and direct entry to the work world. Approximately 66% of all students pursue academic courses, 31% take applied courses, and 2% are enrolled in locally developed courses. Over a 4–5 year period, approximately 96% of students graduate.

Measurement plays a critical role in the work of the staff at Holy Trinity. Both school-based and provincial scores are disaggregated to provide critical evidence for planning around student achievement. Data about credits collected or missed, as well as data about attendance, attitudes, and behaviors, guide intervention strategies. The amount of measurement that occurs at a school the size of Holy Trinity is enormous. As might be expected, some of it yields results that are very gratifying—and some that are less so. The administration and staff celebrate the good news that they find in the data and analyze the brutal facts when they appear in order to plan for improvement. As John said once about some math scores, "The overall result is decent, but we have a distance to go. We will go back to the drawing board and see what we can do!"

Tracking Student Achievement

Holy Trinity works on the semester system. Each semester, achievement data are analyzed at midterm. Struggling students are identified and supports put in place. The school administrators have taken a stand that no final marks from 46–49% are to be given unless the teacher can justify the mark. So far, no one has justified a score in that range. Teachers do what it takes to help students be successful. Tables 5-1 and 5-2 provide school-based data samples that are generated over the course of a semester.

Table 5-1: Success and Failure Information at Midterm

Grade	Credits Attempted	Credits Failed	Number of Credits From 46–49%	Overall Success Rate
9	1,136	39	13	96.6%
10	1,120	66	19	94.1%
11	1,128	75	25	93.3%
12	951	90	18	91.2%
Totals by School	4,335	270	75	93.8%

Table 5-2: Success and Failure Information at the End of the Semester

Grade	Credits Attempted	Credits Failed	Number of Credits From 46–49%	Overall Success Rate
9	1,136	45	0	96.11%
10	1,120	43	0	96.17%
11	1,128	35	0	96.97%
12	951	59	0	93.89%
Totals by School	4,335	182	0	95.79%

One hundred fifty-nine Holy Trinity students are identified as having special needs. Of those, 140 have been assessed through the Identify Placement and Review Committee (IPRC). All special needs students have individualized education programs (IEPs), which outline the special services and supports required to assist them with their learning. Table 5-3 shows the achievement data pertaining to this group of students.

Table 5-3: Achievement Data for Students With Special Needs

	IPRC Students	Students With an IEP
Number of students	141	159
Total attempted credits	517	590.5
Number of successful credits	489.5	560.5
Credits lost	27.5	30
Success rate	94.7%	94.9%

The Education Quality and Accountability Office (EQAO) of the Ontario government is responsible for creating and administering provincial testing at grades 3, 6, 9, and 12. At the high school level, results are disaggregated to provide the scores of students writing academic, applied, and locally developed compulsory courses. Academic courses are those that develop student knowledge and skill in theoretical and abstract areas. Applied courses focus on essential outcomes; they develop student knowledge and skill using practical applications and concrete examples. Locally developed compulsory courses are those that focus on fundamental knowledge and skills that students need to be successful in workplace preparation courses.

Each year, the staff at Holy Trinity sets goals for achievement on the Provincial Assessments. For the 2007–08 year, they set their literacy target at 93%.

Ontario Secondary School Literacy Test Results for 2006–07

All Students–89%

Academic—98%

Applied—72%

Locally Developed—50%

Participating Students—97%

Table 5-4 (page 70) illustrates mathematics scores over a 4-year period. For the 2007–08 school year, the staff at Holy Trinity set their EQAO grade 9 math target at 90%.

Table 5-4: Success Rates for Mathematics, Grades 9 and 10

Course	2003/2004	2004/2005	2005/2006	2006/2007
Grade 9 Applied	78%	81%	89%	83%
Grade 9 Academic	95%	91%	94%	96%
Grade 10 Applied	75%	89%	92%	93%
Grade 10 Academic	88%	89%	86%	94%
Locally Developed Compulsory Credit	90%	85%	100%	100%
EQAO—Academic	87%	70%	80%	75%
EQAO—Applied	29%	54%	43%	62%

Ensuring That No Kid Is Invisible: How Do They Do It?

In keeping with their commitment to ensure that no kid is invisible, the staff has implemented many creative practices and procedures to ensure that all students are known, recognized, and cared for at their school.

1. They do not accept failure as an option.

    *   **The Student Success Team**—This team sometimes calls itself the ALERT Team because their goal is to be alert to what is happening with their students at all times. It plays a critical role in monitoring the academic, social, emotional, and physical needs of students who are identified as at risk. Students are deemed at risk if they achieve 60% or lower in their ongoing classroom-based assessment. The team is comprised of the principal, vice principals, guidance counselors, student success teacher, child youth worker, chaplain, and school social worker. It meets every Tuesday morning. Once students are identified, one of the team members becomes involved to assist the student and monitor progress for the week. Assistance provided may take the form of arranging for extra help, clothing, food, or shelter. Progress is reviewed at the next ALERT meeting, and a team decision is made to continue intensive support or monitor from a distance.

    *   **Mandatory study hall**—Grade 9 and 10 students with class averages lower than 60% in one or more subject areas are required to attend a mandatory study hall on Tuesday, Wednesday, and Thursday for 35 minutes at lunch. There are approximately 100 students enrolled at any given time, and the study hall is staffed

by teacher volunteers from various subjects. Senior students also provide peer tutoring assistance in study hall. Students can earn their way out of study hall by raising their marks sufficiently to demonstrate that they are no longer at risk in that course. There are always at least two math and science teachers available. Currently, 32 teachers are on a rotation for the study hall, and all of them truly believe that failure is not an option for their students. Their success is detailed in Table 5-5. The data presented are for those students assigned to study hall and do not include data for students who drop in for extra help.

Table 5-5: Study Hall Data Analysis for the Second Semester of 2006–07

Number of students enrolled in study hall	120
Number of credits for students enrolled in study hall	137
Number of credits saved	117
Number of credits lost	20
Study hall success rate	85.4%

- **Senior students study hall**—Volunteer teachers of senior classes make themselves available for extra help during the lunch hour on a drop-in basis or by appointment. The study hall becomes mandatory when senior students fail to submit one or more assignments or show evidence that they are struggling and falling behind.

- **Credit recovery**—As part of the Ontario government's Student Success/Learning to 18 Strategy, students who have failed up to three courses can be part of a Credit Recovery Program. The Student Success Teacher at Holy Trinity is a staff member whose time is dedicated to overseeing the Credit Recovery Program by helping students to develop a credit recovery learning plan and supporting them as they work on it.

- **Credit rescue**—The School Success Teacher also works with students who fail a single course with a mark between 40% and 45% in order to help them salvage the credit without summer or night school.

- **Rigorous attention to attendance**—Priority is given to student attendance. The administration and office staff work together to deal with attendance issues before they become serious.

- **Regular, documented teacher contact with parents and care-givers**—Parents and caregivers are alerted when there are concerns about attendance or when mandatory study hall is required.

- **Moodle**—The Modular Object-Oriented Dynamic Learning Environment, or Moodle, is a web-based communication tool on the Holy Trinity website that allows teachers to post information about curriculum (daily and long-term plans), resources, home-work assignments, and other information to help students know what is expected of them in their classes. Moodle also allows students to conduct online discussions with each other and to receive online feedback from their teachers.

- **eLibrary**—All students have access to eLibrary, which grants them electronic access to the major libraries of the world.

2. They focus on student belonging and wellness needs.

- **Extracurricular clubs and sports activities**—Over 20 teachers have organized 21 clubs to address a wide range of interests. These clubs are available to all students at Holy Trinity. Most clubs are run during the lunch hour. The Games Club runs on Monday and Friday (when there is no study hall) so that all students can participate. Twenty-five sports teams are offered with over 30 teachers coaching. A bus provides transportation after extracurricular activities for rural students so that they may participate in the many activities that are offered.

- **Positive transition from grade 8 to 9**—When Holy Trinity staff visit the feeder schools each year to prepare for the intake of new students, they collect information from the current teachers about special abilities, needs, and aptitudes exhibited by students who will be entering grade 9. Grade 8 students are surveyed to determine their interest in extracurricular activities. Based on the survey results, the teachers develop a "giftedness bank," which is a listing of the interests, aptitudes, and special strengths of the students who will be new to the school in the fall. Teachers invite students to attend meetings for clubs and teams that might be of interest to them. Names of incoming students are posted and reviewed by staff to identify those they are working or connecting with outside of class time. The Student Success Team intervenes for students who are not connected to at least one teacher. No child is invisible at Holy Trinity CHS.

- **Peer mentoring**—Any grade 9 student who is at risk is paired with a grade 11 student from a course entitled "Leadership and Peer Mentoring." Mentoring pairs are established so that both students have come from the same feeder school and have shared interests. The grade 11 students receive training about mentorship relationships and are provided with supporting resources. Mentors work with their peers in areas such as literacy building, self-esteem improvement, numeracy skills, artistic skills, organizational skills, and community building activities. The overall goal for the project is to help the younger students become secure enough to take the risks required to learn and become active members of the school community.

- **Socioemotional data collection**—Data are collected from students on social and emotional issues of concern to them. In addition, discipline and attendance data are analyzed with a view to identifying topics of importance to the students. Assemblies are planned at which guest speakers present on topics the students have identified. Examples of assembly topics include bullying, high-risk behaviors, self-esteem and relationship-building, and drug awareness. The ALERT Team works with the rest of the staff to identify and intervene with students who exhibit the need for emotional, behavioral, or physical support.

3. They make professional learning a priority.

- **Collaboration**—Teachers work in teams both within the school and with the other two high schools in the district to analyze test results and address areas needing attention. They collaborate to identify essential learning outcomes and ensure curriculum alignment.

- **Staff surveys**—Each spring, all staff members are surveyed about their personal professional development needs. The results are collated and published along with plans for providing the requested training during the following year.

- **Professional development**—Professional development (PD) is a declared priority at Holy Trinity, and the funds to support training and purchase needed resources are readily available. Time is created during the regular school day for professional development by scheduling sessions around student assemblies. While grades 9 and 10 are in assembly, half of the teachers are in the first PD session. The presentation is repeated for the rest of the staff while grades 11 and 12 are in assembly.

◊ Staff meetings are designed with a 30-minute PD component that is teacher-driven and teacher-delivered. Weekly memos highlight information items that may have otherwise been found on a staff meeting agenda.

◊ Professional growth is enhanced through teachers writing and sharing summaries of books they have read about teaching and learning.

◊ Teachers have formed book clubs to explore best practices in assessment and evaluation. The teachers meet weekly between 3:45 and 6:00 p.m. to study current literature on assessment and identify new approaches to try. They are discovering that changed assessment practice leads to changed instructional practice, and they are supporting each other in the learning process. The first session of the book club involved eight teachers. An additional 10 teachers joined for the second session, and eight more teachers have indicated they will join for the next session. The momentum in this area is growing as teachers share successes and problem solve together.

◊ "Teachers Teaching Teachers" at the school level is an accepted practice at Holy Trinity. Teachers share their expertise with each other through presentations as well as through mentoring relationships.

◊ "Teachers Teaching Teachers" at the board level is a way in which lateral networking and collaboration are encouraged. Professional development days, at which secondary teachers from around the district offer workshops to share their expertise with each other, are organized centrally. At the most recent Board-sponsored PD day, 12 of the 15 sessions offered were presented by teachers from Holy Trinity CHS.

4. They focus on the creation of a school culture that is both caring and vibrant.

- Students televise morning announcements through the Trinity Video Network (TVN). Students assist with creating a professional and collaborative climate in the school by reinforcing values and routines. The singing of *O Canada* followed by a morning prayer is a daily ritual at Holy Trinity. Respecting and listening to the morning announcements is an established norm in the school.

- It is also a norm that interaction between staff members is professional and positive. Motivational artwork lines the hallways, emphasizing the key components of character education.

- Staff members demonstrate unparalleled willingness to support each other around instructional and extracurricular initiatives. Participation in the county fair builds tradition through hard work and participation in sports, arts, and community-building activities.

- There is a strong, whole-school focus on two critical aspects of social responsibility: charity and justice. Students and staff at Holy Trinity believe, as Mahatma Gandhi once said, that they must be the change they want to see in the world. To that end, they are involved in numerous prosocial activities such as food drives, community clean-up initiatives, self-esteem workshops for girls, Earth Day activities, and AIDS awareness, to name only a few.

- The school is kept in spotless condition. There is no evidence of graffiti, and lockers are clean.

- School photos and student artwork are prominently displayed to further celebrate the school community.

- Staff are highly visible in the hallways to support and interact with students.

Moving Forward With Pride

In conversation with John Burroughs, the pride he feels for the accomplishments achieved by the staff of Holy Trinity Catholic High School is clearly evident. He holds high expectations for both staff and students and is passionate in his intention to do whatever it takes to ensure learning for all.

C. J. Schurter School

C. J. Schurter School is located in Slave Lake, a northern Alberta town. According to information provided by the school, Slave Lake was identified by Statistics Canada in the 2006 census as one of the 10 youngest communities in Canada. With a population of 7,031, Slave Lake has grown rapidly due to active lumber, gas, and oil industries. As the population has grown, many new retail businesses have opened. Along with booming lumber, gas, and oil industries, this has caused a shortage of workers and housing. Slave Lake is a very transient town, with people moving frequently from many different communities in the northern part of the province.

The school houses 430 students from kindergarten to grade 3. There are five or six classes at each grade level and about 20 students in each class. A significant percentage of the student population exhibits complex learning and/or social emotional needs. Transience seriously disrupts learning for large numbers of students each year. There are 48 staff, of which 28 are teachers and 20 are support staff.

Identifying Shared Beliefs and Values

Robyn Ord-Boisvert became the principal of C. J. Schurter School in 2004, upon the retirement of the previous principal, who had been there for 32 years. Robyn knew going in that it would be difficult to make changes to existing programs and structures and that she would need to acknowledge and respect the existing culture of the school. She felt strongly, however, that it was her responsibility to provide the leadership necessary to facilitate a cultural shift that would enhance student achievement.

Using the effective schools correlates as their guide, Robyn and the vice principal, Nancy MacDonald, began working with the staff. They started with discussion about their moral purpose as educators and moved on to articulating the beliefs and values that were shared by all. In the first year of what they refer to as their effective schools journey, the staff formally revisited and reinforced their school values on four different occasions. Since then, they have had several professional development sessions devoted to the affirmation, clarification, enhancement, and celebration of the statements that were generated. Staff retreats have been held away from the school in order to have time to reflect on their collective progress in relation to their stated beliefs and values. This reflection has reinforced the shared beliefs and values and renewed commitment to enhancing them.

The beliefs and values identified by Robyn and the staff provide the foundation upon which all decisions are made at C. J. Schurter. Budget priorities, new resources, and staffing considerations are all filtered through them. Hiring practices have shifted dramatically to focus on finding individuals who fit with the school values and improvement initiatives. The staff's shared beliefs and values serve to focus all their work as a professional learning community (PLC) and provide a common language for prioritizing goals and initiatives. They are also reflected in the school song, daily morning announcements, calendars, and newsletters. The staff of C. J. Schurter live their values on a daily basis.

Making Measurement Matter

With their beliefs and values clearly articulated, the staff embraced a solid school improvement planning process for which measurement and the collection, disaggregation, and analysis of data are the driving forces. Their collaborative work and professional learning have been guided by what the measurements have revealed.

While the focus on measurement has proven to be a powerful tool, Robyn and her staff also say that it has been a source of struggle and great frustration at times because of the changes it precipitated. It has forced them to critically examine their assessment practice and curricular benchmarks, tools and resources, and administration procedures.

As their curricular understanding grew, so did their understanding about assessment and data collection. New insights about the essential outcomes at each grade level compelled the staff to investigate new assessment tools and practices. The staff found that the more they learned about grade-level benchmarks, the higher their expectations became, and the higher the achievement bar was raised. Continuous reflection and re-evaluation resulted in changes to programs, resources, and delivery models, as well as assessment practices and methods of data collection. Changes in assessment practice have led to changes to report cards and reporting practices. As they worked, a momentum built that compelled them to keep moving forward.

In the 4 years that they have been on this journey together, the staff of C. J. Schurter have acquired a professional confidence they did not have before. They now verbalize that they feel professionally accountable to their students, parents, each other, and themselves. In Robyn's words, "Though the work is hard and frustrating at times, the end results are well worth the effort. We are changing the lives of children every day!"

Provincial Assessment

Grade 3 students in Alberta write Provincial Achievement Tests each spring. The entire staff shares the responsibility for the outcomes, regardless of the grade they teach. The grade 3 provincial standards and benchmarks have been used to map backwards and to identify benchmarks at each grade beginning with kindergarten. These benchmarks inform the instruction in all classes. Without exception, all teachers at C.J. Schurter recognize the part they play in the achievement of their grade 3 students.

A strong classroom-based assessment program serves to inform instruction on a daily basis and provides solid support for achievement of the standards tested through the provincial assessment program. Reading achievement in all grades is assessed and monitored using the PM Benchmark Kit, a commercial reading assessment resource. To enhance writing instruction, grade-level PLC teams have developed continua that identify grade-level writing benchmarks. Exemplars and rubrics have been developed to help students understand their writing targets, reflect on their progress, and plan for improvement. As Table 5-6 shows, the staff have seen substantial improvement in provincial test results as a result of their efforts over the 3-year period from 2003 to 2006.

Table 5-6: C. J. Schurter Provincial Achievement Test Results

	2003–04	2004–05	2005–06
Language Arts			
Participation Rate	90.7%	91.0%	92.9%
Acceptable	79.4%	84.0%	91.2%
Excellent	6.2%	11.1%	15.4%
Below Acceptable	20.6%	16.0%	8.8%
Math			
Participation Rate	89.7%	92.1%	91.8%
Acceptable	75.0%	84.1%	92.2%
Excellent	12.5%	25.6%	25.6%
Below Acceptable	25.0%	15.9%	7.8%

School-Based Assessment

SMART goals guide instruction in reading and writing. Critical evidence is collected at each grade level in November, March, and June to monitor student progress toward the goals. Common assessment tools are used. Tables 5-7 and 5-8 show a sample of the June 2006 data for each grade.

Table 5-7: Performance on Grade-Level Reading Benchmark

	Percentage of Students Achieving Grade-Level Reading Benchmark
Grade 1	69%
Grade 2	72%
Grade 3	87%

Table 5-8: Performance on Grade-Level Writing Benchmark

	Percentage of Students Achieving Grade-Level Writing Benchmark
Grade 1	59%
Grade 2	57%
Grade 3	75%

How Did They Do It?

1. They developed a positive, collaborative culture.

   - An effective schools team consisting of the administrators and staff representatives was established to serve as a liaison between grade levels and overall school planning.

   - School and grade-level PLCs have set SMART goals to guide their planning.

   - The staff made learning how to use measurement data effectively a priority.

   - Grade-level PLCs meet once or twice a month during the school day to do the following:

     ◊ Develop long-range plans for the school in mathematics and language arts.

     ◊ Identify and monitor student achievement benchmarks for reading and writing.

     ◊ Develop grade-level reporting procedures based on benchmarks.

◊ Analyze measurement data to determine what it means for their instruction.

◊ Collaborate to plan skill-boosting instruction for students who are not meeting the benchmarks.

- PLC meetings are formalized and include agendas, minutes, and norms.

- Monthly staff meetings include discussion and celebration of the work being done by the grade-level PLCs.

- Teachers have taken ownership of all students in the school, not just those in their classrooms. They view Provincial Achievement Tests in grade 3 as a joint responsibility and have worked as a team toward raising their scores.

- Assessment data are used to group students at each grade level to provide daily skill boosts for students not meeting benchmarks in reading and writing.

- Literacy and math celebrations are part of monthly assemblies.

2. They made improved instruction and the use of high-yield strategies a priority.

- Data have been disaggregated to clearly identify the current reality and to target students who struggle.

- Baseline data are collected for all students, and achievement is monitored over time. Periodic reassessments are used to gauge growth along the way.

- Improved assessment tools are being used.

- All in-class and home reading books have been organized according to reading level so that students at all levels have books available to them.

- Skill boosts are provided at all grades for students who are achieving below grade level. Two Boost Teachers work with groups of four to six students for 15–20 minutes daily on skills that need a boost.

- Teachers collaborate to share students between them as instructional groups are created to cluster students with similar needs for part of each day.

- Parent volunteers provide in-class support to teachers so that they can work with students individually or in small groups.

- The first 25 minutes of each day are devoted to independent reading time.

- Staff have adopted a balanced literacy approach to language arts instruction.

- Resources have been purchased to support instruction.

- Grade-level writing rubrics and exemplars have been developed.

3. Professional learning is focused and continuous.

When they embarked on their effective schools journey, teachers scrambled to get the professional development they felt they needed. The sheer volume of professional development inherent in their renewed focus on instruction and improved achievement created a sense of uncertainty within the staff. Some became overwhelmed; others became impatient; and still others lost confidence and just wanted to be told what to do. The staff needed to step back and assess the impact this increased professional development workload was having on the school environment. Through discussion, the staff decided to bring coherence to their efforts by consolidating professional development opportunities into manageable chunks. A schoolwide approach to professional development was adopted, and professional learning was embedded in the day-to-day work of the school. The effect was positive:

- AISI (Alberta Initiative for School Improvement) leaders have been included as integral partners on the C. J. Schurter learning journey and work regularly with the staff.

- Literacy and math coaches were contracted to work with the staff to share, model, and assist with understanding and using high-yield strategies, best practices, and essential learnings.

- PLC work is viewed as a powerful form of professional development.

- All individual teacher growth plans are aligned with the school plan.

- New and absent staff are brought up to speed using video recordings of professional development sessions.

Looking Back With Satisfaction

Robyn recently shared what she called an "aha moment" that occurred as she was reflecting on her time as principal of C. J. Schurter School. These are her words:

> During the past 4 years, our school has adopted many new strategies and approaches that have contributed to enhanced student achievement. Our journey did not involve the immediate adoption of one high-yield strategy; but rather, it included several small, supported changes that served both as a catalyst to larger, more complex changes and as an opportunity to reflect on instructional practice and resource selection.

Robyn and the staff of C. J. Schurter School have many reasons to be proud of the work they have done together.

Chimo Elementary School

Located in Smith Falls, Ontario, Chimo Elementary is a junior kindergarten to grade 8 school with a population of 358. The staff consists of 20.6 fulltime equivalent teachers and eight and a half educational assistants. Smith Falls demographics indicate that the average wage in that area is below the average Canadian fulltime wage, and the median family income is also below the national norm. Two major industries in the area will be closing soon, and this will have a significant negative financial impact on the municipality.

Laurie McCabe became the principal of Chimo Elementary in 2004. Under her leadership, the Chimo staff became very conscious of the importance of data in their work. A comprehensive measurement program was established to provide the information they need to inform their work in the classroom, as well as their practice in the areas of student deportment and professional development.

Establishing a Safe and Orderly Environment

The 2004–05 school year was Laurie's first at Chimo and first as a principal. Over the course of that year, she became concerned about the number of discipline referrals and suspensions they were dealing with. She observed that suspensions were not resulting in changed behavior. In addition, a virtues-based character education initiative had been implemented, but she was not seeing carryover in student behavior. After analyzing discipline data, she noted that many of the problems staff were dealing with were virtue related. There was a negative tone in the school, and a lot of apathy was apparent in some areas. Staff were frustrated with student disregard for expected behaviors and attitudes and frequently sent students to the office to be dealt with by administration.

Character Education Virtues	
• Respect	• Caring
• Resiliency	• Empathy
• Perseverance	• Responsibility
• Fairness	• Honesty

Laurie shared her observations and concerns with the staff. As a result, a staff committee worked with her to develop an intervention plan. By June 2005, the groundwork was laid for a new approach to discipline at Chimo to be instituted the next school year.

The new strategy involved all staff, including office administrators, custodians, and other support staff, in adopting a unified approach to their work with the kids. The philosophy espoused in the book *With All Due Respect: Keys for Building Effective School Discipline* (Morrish, 2000) was combined with a renewed focus on the virtues embedded in the Character Education program and resulted in the following changes:

- Staff engaged in in-depth discussion and extensive training about strategies for supporting students and staff when discipline is the issue.

- Expectations were raised for students and staff.

- Much effort was put into developing a team perspective in which the staff shares responsibly for all students in the school, regardless of which class they are in.

- The school shifted its focus from intervention (dealing with failure to behave) to prevention (teaching students how to behave).

- Communication with students, staff, and parents about behavioral expectations was carried out in a variety of ways on an ongoing basis.

- The staff adopted a positive, consistent approach to expectations.

- Teachers became the key players in teaching students to behave appropriately.

- Teachers and staff members dealt with critical issues immediately.

- The role of administrators shifted to one of support for teachers in working with students to help them understand and be successful in living up to the stated expectations.

- Adults adopted the attitude that it *is* important to sweat the small stuff.

- Character education virtues were combined with training for appropriate behaviors.

- Assemblies were held to highlight character virtues.

- Virtues were embedded in instruction and instructional approaches (such as quality daily physical education, differentiated instruction, multiple intelligences, learning styles, and so on).

Over the course of the 2005–06 school year, the number of students suspended at Chimo Elementary went from 187 to fewer than 15, and the number of students sent to the office for behavioral reasons also decreased dramatically. The tone of the school improved significantly, with students and teachers greeting each other in the hallways and interacting informally. Students demonstrated improved manners and behaviors; teachers were more involved in supporting student deportment; and early intervention to prevent and rectify concerns had become the norm. Actively teaching appropriate behavior and attitudes has paid big dividends at Chimo Elementary.

Gathering Critical Evidence About Student Achievement

As with all schools in Ontario, Chimo students are required to participate in the provincial testing program at grades 3 and 6. Based on EQAO results, a Chimo School Success Plan was developed using SMART goals to guide assessment and instruction practice. Classroom-based assessment *for* learning is done at each grade level to provide baseline and interim monitoring information.

Baseline assessment on each student is collected each September using the PM Benchmark Kit at the primary level and another commercial product, CASI (Comprehension, Attitudes, Strategies, and Interests) at the junior and intermediate levels. In addition, a mathematics diagnostics test in number sense and numeration is used at all levels. Students are assessed using the same instruments periodically throughout the year to track their progress, and updated scores are recorded during the winter term and again during the spring term.

School opening assessment results are used to create a data wall at the primary level by having each teacher use a different color of sticky note to place his or her students on a tracking board according to their reading level. This creates a visual display of student reading levels that teachers use to form reading groups and provide instruction at appropriate levels for all students. More frequent and student-specific running records are also kept for all grade 1 students. The results are used to place them in flexible groupings two or three times a week for small-group instruction to focus on improving reading levels.

Class profiles at all grade levels are completed early in the school year. The profiles record critical evidence about the strengths, weaknesses, and program accommodations required for each student in the class. They also include information about each student's learning style preference, multiple intelligence strengths, PM Benchmark reading level (for primary), CASI strengths and needs (for junior/intermediate), and general interests. Interests are determined by individually interviewing each student. Learning styles and multiple intelligence strengths are determined using related inventories. Profiles are kept current by updating them during the winter and spring terms based on new data about each student's achievement.

Working within the PLC context is the accepted practice at Chimo Elementary, and all PLC teams have established norms and purposes related to instruction. Minutes are kept, and school leaders attend the meetings. The work of the professional learning community centers on understanding curriculum and improving instruction. Assessment data are analyzed and used to inform next steps according to the SMART goals that have been set. Many other positive outcomes can be attributed to the impact of teachers working within PLCs: A strong team dynamic has developed, virtues education has been enhanced, and teacher morale has improved.

Professional Learning

Professional learning at Chimo is aligned with school goals outlined in the School Success Plan and teachers' annual learning plans that have been

Grid for Class Profiles

Name _____

Individualized Education Plan _____

Accommodations _____

Modifications_____

Learning Style Preference_____

Multiple Intelligence Strengths _____

Reading Level _____

CASI Strengths/Needs _____

Interests_____

developed. A gap analysis staff survey provides important information for planning professional development activities at the school. The survey identifies areas of required collective growth and asks teachers to reflect on their individual level of comfort with each. To support teachers in their professional growth, creative timetabling allows teachers to be released during the school day for 40 minutes once a week. Additionally, 30 minutes of staff meeting time are devoted to sharing information obtained at workshops and PLC meetings. The introduction to the survey reads as follows:

> Please fill out the attached survey so that we can plan for professional development and provide support where needed for next year. Please indicate your **comfort level** with each initiative and how you would like to learn about it so it becomes a "habit" in your classroom.
>
> **Cushy Chair** = High level of understanding, using in classroom on a frequent and regular basis
>
> **Wooden Bench** = Familiar with concept, only dabbling, haven't put it into practice regularly
>
> **Bed of Nails** = Sounds familiar, not sure what it means or looks like, not doing it, haven't read it

The survey also asks teachers to identify their preferred method of receiving the required training: on their own, one to one, in a small group, modeled by staff, class observation, or other. Based on the survey results, professional development opportunities are developed and implemented. Learning opportunities are advertised through invitations that are posted next to *Chimo Chatter,* the staff communication newsletter that is posted daily in the staff room.

Staff Survey Categories

- General interest professional reading
- Professional reading pertaining to literacy
- Resources (curriculum supports and AV resources)
- Ministry documents
- Instructional strategies and best practices
- Assessment and evaluation
- Information and assistive technology
- Special interest topics (noncrisis intervention, autism, CPR, first aid, and so on)

Looking Back With Satisfaction

Laurie transferred in 2008 to a school closer to her home. In her time at Chimo, Laurie's leadership and effective use of measurement made a significant difference to the school climate and environment for student learning. The staff grew in its ability to work collaboratively, and positive growth in student achievement was reflected in the EQAO results. Most importantly, the students at Chimo benefited from improved instruction in academic, social, emotional, and behavioral domains.

Summary

"Frequent monitoring of student progress" is integral to the process of planning to improve. While this may seem threatening or confusing to staff at first, in the final analysis, it is absolutely critical if improved school and student success is truly a priority. A multitude of measurement tools are available for classroom use. They must be selected based on their ability to provide useful information about individual student achievement.

Teachers can determine what information will be useful only by knowing the curriculum and identifying essential learnings. External measurements also serve a useful, albeit different, purpose. They provide needed big-picture information for schools and divisions about instruction and the achievement of standards. The relative importance of data yielded through various forms of measurement is dependent upon the perspective of the people analyzing them. In every respect, however, measurement is a critical component of the collaborative work that is the highlight of the lesson presented in chapter 6.

If at First You Don't Succeed . . .
Do Whatever It Takes

Uncertainty is inherent in teaching. Today's classrooms are filled with students with multiple needs, and schools are being challenged to ensure that all students succeed. The issues that educators must grapple with are adaptive challenges for which the solutions lie outside the current way of operating. Theories abound that suggest how these dilemmas might be addressed, but while they provide us with direction, they may not translate into practice as easily as we would like. Local conditions, organizational culture, leadership, community expectations, and other factors can interfere with even the most carefully crafted plans. Teachers working together with an attitude of doing whatever it takes to achieve learning by all are the key to success. Working with this mindset, teachers can hold high expectations for students as well as themselves—knowing that they will persist until they find a way to make success possible.

The notion of collaboration has become embedded in current educational thinking, and the power of collaborative school cultures in addressing today's educational challenges is widely recognized. We should not, however, consider an understanding of the concept of collaboration and teacher willingness to engage a foregone conclusion. For many years, teachers have been accustomed to working in isolation. They have enjoyed a lot of autonomy. Congeniality has been prized over collegiality. Experience tells us that authentic collaboration requires that teacher paradigms about the work that needs to be done and the means of doing it effectively must shift. True collaboration requires that teachers create knowledge together through examining current data about student achievement and engaging in joint planning to address identified gaps. Cultures built on collaboration are characterized by job-embedded professional growth, continuous learning, and collective responsibility for accountability. The skills of working collaboratively must be learned and practiced in a culture that values inquiry and action research.

Collaborative teams committed to a shared vision of learning by all hold high expectations for success for students and themselves. They approach their work knowing that they may have to make in-flight corrections along the way to help them meet their goals. They know that often there is more than one way to approach a problem. Working with a mindset of continuous improvement, they celebrate victories as they achieve them. Collaborative teams are characterized by a spirit of inquiry in which failures are seen as opportunities to learn. They are motivated by the understanding that if at first you don't succeed . . . you must do whatever it takes. They also understand that it is imperative to create a school environment that is safe, orderly, and conducive to taking the risks required to learn.

Building collaborative teams takes time, effort, and persistence. Developing plans also takes time and effort. Successfully implementing them takes commitment, creativity, intuition, and—sometimes—courage. Creating a school culture that is characterized by authentic collaboration is an adaptive challenge that requires that the people involved accept the need to change and be willing to learn new ways. To achieve this, the existing equilibrium must be disturbed—but only at a rate that people can absorb. A safe and orderly environment and effective leadership are critical.

The Link to Effective Schools Research

"High expectations for success" is a correlate that applies to both students and teachers. It must be understood, however, that high expectations without the necessary learning and support to ensure that they can be met are sure to lead to discouragement and feelings of hopelessness. Sometimes finding the best instructional strategies and supports is not as easy as it looks on the surface.

Lezotte and McKee (2002) explained that high expectations are most likely to be met in an atmosphere that is "orderly, purposeful and business-like . . . free from the threat of physical harm." They describe a climate that is conducive to teaching and learning as being free from "oppression," distinguished by "strong student academic and social engagement" (p. 18). A safe and orderly environment is a prerequisite for learning.

A major challenge that teachers must address is students who do not learn, in spite of the fact that their teachers have had, and acted upon, high expectations. Lezotte and McKee (2002) explained that for high expectations for student and teacher success to be realistic, schools must be "transformed from institutions designed for instruction to institutions designed to assure learning" (p. 205). To do that, high expectations must be gauged by staff beliefs and behaviors as well as by the school's response when some students do not learn. Lezotte and McKee presented this scenario for consideration: If teachers plan and deliver a lesson, assess learning, and—even after finding that some students did not learn—go on to the next lesson anyway, it's fair to conclude they did not really expect the students to learn in the first place. They went on to say that when schools condone this practice through silence, they apparently also do not expect students to learn—or teachers to teach, for that matter.

Effective schools research tells us that high expectations for student success must be launched from a platform of high expectations for teacher and, ultimately, school success. Teachers must expand their knowledge base as well as their repertoire of instructional strategies to meet the diverse needs of their students; however, schools must also respond by revamping existing structures and practices to assure that teachers have access to the tools and supports they need in their efforts to do so. As Lezotte and McKee (2002) said, "Teachers cannot implement most of these strategies working alone in isolated classrooms" (p. 204). It is only when the entire school shifts its focus from teaching to learning and problem-solving that is shared by all stakeholders that high expectations for success for all will be a realistic goal.

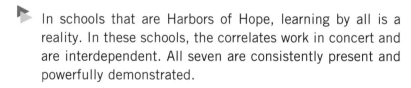 In schools that are Harbors of Hope, learning by all is a reality. In these schools, the correlates work in concert and are interdependent. All seven are consistently present and powerfully demonstrated.

What We Have Learned About the Lesson

The only way to assure that high expectations for success are a reality is to remove failure as an option. If students are allowed to fail, some will. Removing failure as an option is a big commitment to make, and there are bound to be some who will identify obstacles deemed to be insurmountable. There are those who will blame lack of student motivation (they aren't holding up their end of the bargain), and others will say that too much hand-holding just enables irresponsible behavior. Some will blame the home, saying that there is inadequate support because parents are either not interested or make excuses for their kids.

The truth is, these insurmountable barriers are nothing more than excuses for not making the commitment to success for all. It is true that conditions for students outside of the school sometimes get in the way of school success. As educators, we cannot alter those conditions. We can, however, affect school conditions to allow for each student's skill level, strengths, and learning style. We can use the best possible instructional strategies and give students the support they need to remove failure as an option. To do this requires that educators take a problem-solving stance and work collectively at removing barriers to learning, creating new approaches to replace those that are no longer effective, and thinking hard about how to make it possible for *all* students to succeed.

Craig Jerald (2003) wrote about a "peeling the onion" problem-solving approach to improving classroom and organizational practice. According to him, peeling the onion means that "rather than attempting to solve all problems at once or trying to cram an externally designed system into place, administrators and teachers identify immediate obstacles and tackle them first" (p. 16). His observation was that as solutions are found and success is experienced, new sets of challenges and obstacles present themselves, and the work becomes increasingly deep and sophisticated. Jerald maintained that until educators begin asking "fundamental questions (peeling the onion) to directly confront what's working and what's not, they will remain stuck between a rock and a hard place" (p. 16). Such fundamental questions revolve around how to respond to students who are at risk of falling behind and what to do for students who are not learning. Consideration of these questions leads to an examination of time, space, staffing arrangements, and instructional approaches. Little by little, the instructional onion is peeled, and the school becomes more responsive to student needs.

Smart Conversations to Make a Difference

Smart Meetings, a process developed by Bob Wiele, founder and chief innovation officer of One Smart World, Inc., provides a structure to ensure that all voices are heard and joint planning becomes a reality. Using the Smart Meeting format, team meetings result in people making a commitment to action and arriving at the next meeting prepared to discuss what they have done.

The Smart Meeting format employs thinking strategies based on the traffic light. Red indicates the need to stop, make a decision, and choose a course of action. Yellow means slow down to share ideas and information so that good decisions can be made. Green signals creative thinking and searching for new ideas. Because white contains all of the colors, it determines the level of each individual's personal spirit. Personal spirit, a measurement of commitment and willingness to work to make a difference, is encompassed in white thinking.

A typical Smart Meeting would operate on a yellow-red-green-red-white cycle.

- **Yellow track**—The team shares information based on data and research as well as personal perspectives about what needs to be done to address an identified challenge.

- **Red track**—The team chooses one of the ideas or approaches identified to be the focus of further discussion.

- **Green track**—The team brainstorms ideas as to how the idea or approach chosen could be implemented.

- **Red track**—The team selects methods of implementation for the identified idea or approach being considered.

- **White track**—Each team member states specifically what they will do to assist with implementation and their level of commitment to the action.

At the next Smart Meeting, during the yellow track discussion, members of the team report their observations about what they tried during the yellow track discussion—and the cycle begins again. Principal support and leadership are required to implement and sustain the Smart Meeting process. When team members do not engage or commit, they create an excellent opportunity for discussion and, if necessary, performance contracting.

Knowing What It Takes—and Doing It

Carol Ann Tomlinson (2003) has cited six principles for fostering equity and excellence in academically diverse learners.

- The teacher's primary responsibility is to ensure a coherent, relevant, engaging, and thoughtful curriculum.

- All students deserve to know which knowledge, understandings, and skills are the targets for each lesson. They should be required to use the higher order thinking skills they are capable of and should find the work interesting and compelling.

- The best instruction stretches students just a bit beyond their comfort levels. Supports must be in place to assist them with achieving success in the challenges presented to them.

- Groupings that are flexible and temporary in nature are the key. To accommodate diverse learning needs and styles, ways and time must be found for the class to work as a whole as well as for students to work both alone and with varied groups of peers. Grouping must be flexible in order to avoid labeling students and to provide differentiated fast-track instruction to help them catch up or to extend their learning, depending upon their needs in each subject area.

- Assessment is, in fact, learning. Everything that students do or say provides assessment data. It must be an ongoing process and maximize opportunities for all students to understand and engage in their own learning.

- Teachers are responsible for guiding and supporting students as they work to become the best they can be. Grading should reflect student growth.

Six Principles

Good curriculum comes first.

All tasks should respect each learner.

When in doubt, teach up!

Use flexible grouping.

Become an assessment junkie.

Grade to reflect growth.

(Tomlinson, 2003, p. 9)

DuFour, DuFour, Eaker, and Karhanek (2004) contended that the perceptions that teachers have about their own personal and collective ability to help all students learn are much more significant than their perceptions of student ability to learn. They asserted that educators working together to develop their collective capacity to address student needs is what will develop a sense of self-efficacy—a "belief that it is within their sphere of influence to impact student achievement in a positive way" (p. 182). They called upon teachers to build individual and collective efficacy through working collaboratively to understand and meet the needs of students. And they stressed the importance of creating an intervention system that ensures that effective supports are provided when students require them.

There is overwhelming consensus in the educational literature that working together in a professional learning community (PLC) is the key to addressing the many challenges facing teachers today. DuFour et al. (2006) identified critical questions to guide the work of PLCs, the first two of which are:

1. What is it we want our students to learn?

2. How will we know when each student has learned it? (p. 46)

Characteristics of Professional Learning Communities

- Shared mission, vision, values, and goals

- Collaborative teams

- Collective inquiry

- Action orientation and experimentation

- Continuous improvement

- Results orientation

(DuFour et al., 2004)

Teachers working collaboratively to determine essential learnings, plan instruction, and collect and analyze pertinent achievement data will learn the answers to these questions and will, as a result, be able to recognize when students need more support than they are presently receiving. According to DuFour et al. (2004), when considering its response to students who are experiencing difficulty, a school that purports to be a PLC should be able to answer the following questions in the affirmative (we give our responses in italic):

- Is our response based on INTERVENTION rather than remediation?

  [The plan provides students with extra time and support when they need it, as opposed to after they have failed.]

- Is our response SYSTEMATIC?

  [A schoolwide intervention plan is identified, and the response to students who struggle is consistent.]

- Is our response TIMELY?

  [Extra time and support for learning are provided as soon as students are identified as not learning.]

- Is our response DIRECTIVE?

  [When students are experiencing difficulty, extra time and support for learning are not optional—they are required.]

(DuFour et al., 2004, p. 7)

It Is Not Easy

As teachers collaborate to understand and address the challenges they are confronted with in their work, at times they will feel stuck—as though their best efforts are not making the differences they hoped and planned for. Michael Fullan (2001) called this phenomenon the *implementation dip* and described it as a "dip in performance and confidence as one encounters an innovation that requires new skills and new understandings" (p. 40). Through his research, Fullan has identified a second trend that results in stalled efforts, which he describes as reaching a plateau.

With a team of colleagues from the Ontario Institute for Studies in Education, Fullan evaluated the National Literacy and Numeracy Strategies reform movement in England over a 5-year period from 1997 to 2002. The team made the following observations, which provide invaluable insight into the change process required to ensure learning by all:

1. It is possible, with appropriate pressure and support and a direct focus on literacy and numeracy, to achieve a boost of improvement.

2. Even with enormous effort and substantial financial input, only a minority of schools and districts were deeply engaged in the effort to close the achievement gap.

3. The results plateau well below acceptable levels after a sharp increase between 1997 and 2000. In the 3 years following, results remained at the same level.

4. Good results are not sustainable because it is impossible to sustain the tremendous energy and steep learning curve over an extended period of time. Burnout, overload, and turnover take their toll. As well, motivation flags dramatically when results plateau, and it takes the same great energy just to stand still.

5. There is no evidence that student ability to learn has significantly increased simply as a result of there being more students who are literate and numerate.

6. Centrally driven (top down) reform may be a necessary first step when performance is seriously below par; however, it will never be sufficient to sustain improvement.

What is needed now and for the future is students who have acquired "the ability to learn how to learn and other meta-cognitive or 'thinking' skills; the ability to learn on the job and in teams; the ability to cope with ambiguous situations and unpredictable problems; the ability to communicate well verbally, not just in writing; and the ability to be creative, innovative and entrepreneurial" (Hargreaves, 2003, p. 30).

The Importance of the Balcony

Sometimes, in the midst of a lot of action involving a lot of people, there comes a point when the only recourse is to withdraw from the action to get a new perspective. Heifetz and Linsky (2002) call this phenomenon "getting off the dance floor and going to the balcony." It's an image that they use to capture the "mental activity of stepping back in the midst of action and asking, 'What's really going on here?'" (p. 52). The view from the balcony can help determine who the key players are, what stakes they bring to the issue, and what has to be done to make progress. Because leadership is improvisational, it cannot be scripted. It is only through detached thinking that leaders can accurately assess, reflect, and plan.

Effective leaders realize that retreating to the balcony helps to achieve a clearer view of reality and a renewed perspective on the bigger picture. They also realize that they must return to the dance floor in order to intervene and bring coherence to the work being done. The challenge in this strategy is to move between the dance floor and balcony, make interventions, and then observe their impact. Heifetz and Linsky (2002) continued to tell us that "the goal is to come as close as you can to being in both places simultaneously, as if you had one eye looking from the dance floor and one eye looking down from the balcony watching all the action, including your own" (p. 54). It is not an easy thing for people to see themselves objectively and accurately gauge their impact on others; however, for anyone wishing to influence others, it is an important skill to develop.

Sustaining efforts to meet the needs of diverse learners and, in the process, shift the culture of the school sufficiently to embed new practices requires explicit support. When staff appear to be inundated, besieged, or just plain stuck, it is critical that those in leadership positions get on the balcony to assess the situation and find out what is going on. It is equally important that they return to the dance floor to respond to what they find:

- Are the challenges being encountered technical or adaptive? If they are technical, it is possible to obtain the expert support that is required to address them. If they are adaptive, it is necessary to identify the issue for the staff as a whole and engage them in joint problem-solving or peeling the educational onion, as noted earlier in this chapter.

- How are people feeling? If enthusiasm and energy are flagging, it is important to back off and make time for new learning to be consolidated. Alternatively, perhaps the path presently being followed is not working for the group. It may be time to redirect and file a new flight plan. Sometimes new resources, public acknowledgment of effort, and celebration of achievements to date are required.

- What are people saying? Are they expressing what they really mean? It is possible that people who are complaining are simply reacting to their anxiety about not feeling competent to do what they are being asked to do. People who appear to be resistant may really be just cautious and need extra time to build their confidence to deal with new ways. Heifetz and Linsky caution those in leadership positions to "listen to the song beneath the words" (2002, p. 55).

- What is happening at the district level? What pressures are staff members dealing with? How is it affecting the work that must be done at the school level? Do those in authority know the work that is being done at the school? What could district leaders do to support the school's efforts? How can optimal communication with district administrators be achieved?

Effective leadership requires extensive knowledge and skill. It also requires remarkable intuitive power, because what happens from moment to moment, day to day, is not predictable. Being able to work between the balcony and the dance floor is a critical skill for those in leadership positions to cultivate.

Doing Whatever It Takes

High expectations for all students can be a reality if the learning levels and needs of all students are known. When teachers consistently monitor their students' progress and a system is in place to ensure that they receive the extra help they need when they need it, high expectations for success are justified. High expectations can also be a reality for teachers. Working within a PLC context is the means to developing the knowledge and professional efficacy needed to ensure that all students can live up to the high expectations held for them. In the final analysis, what is important is an organizational mindset that supports doing whatever it takes to make high expectations for student and teacher success both fair and achievable.

What the Lesson Teaches Us

- To effectively address today's educational challenges, teachers must hold high expectations for themselves and their students and commit to doing whatever it takes to reach them.

- Holding high expectations for success is unfair if the required learning and supports are not provided to make the attainment possible.

- Educational theories serve to inform and guide; however, implementation of those theories is often not as easy as it sounds.

- Collaboration is the key to finding solutions to adaptive challenges.

- Collaboration itself is an adaptive challenge, because it requires teacher paradigms to shift away from working in isolation toward working in collegial teams to find solutions to problems.

- A collaborative culture takes time to develop.

- The Smart Meeting strategy provides a process for engaging teachers in joint planning and collaboration.

- Differentiated instruction is necessary to meet diverse learning needs.

- An effective assessment plan uses a variety of methods and has the primary goal of engaging students in their own learning.

- Teacher perceptions of their own efficacy at meeting student needs are more important than their perceptions of student ability to learn.

- Professional learning communities answer these key questions: What is it we want our students to learn? How will we know when each student has learned it?

- A collective problem-solving stance is required to find solutions to addressing the needs of students who are not learning or are at risk of falling behind.

- A systematic, timely, and consistently implemented intervention system for students who struggle is a critical component of meeting high expectations for success.

- As teachers work to implement plans developed to ensure that high expectations for success can be realized, they are likely to experience implementation dips and plateaus that, if left unaddressed, are likely to derail improvement efforts.

- At regular points in the change process, it is critical to back off to allow people time to reenergize and consolidate new learning.

- It is important to divide the work being done into smaller segments in order to set up quick wins that will encourage efforts to continue.

- Celebration of wins and progress made is very important.

- It is reasonable to expect to have to make in-flight corrections to plans as work proceeds and the need to modify is identified.

- Effective leaders know how to work simultaneously between the balcony and the dance floor to ascertain what is happening and what is required for next steps. They scan the environment to a) determine if challenges being encountered are technical or adaptive; b) find out how people are feeling; c) listen to the song beneath the words; and d) learn what is happening at the district level.

- Effective leadership involves knowledge, skills, and strong intuitive abilities. It is as much an art as it is a craft.

Lessons Lived: Stories From the Real World

Schools that make a difference realize that sometimes it is necessary to try again and again to discover what it takes to create the culture and climate that ensures learning by all. The three stories that follow illustrate the power of creative thinking, shared leadership, and persistence in doing whatever it takes to make school and student success a reality.

Vancouver Technical Secondary School

The Globe and Mail (Hume, Dec. 2, 2003, p. A21) listed Vancouver Technical Secondary School as the "most ethnically diverse school in Canada." The school has a population of 1,650 students, of which 280 students have special needs and 140 are First Nations. The school houses students from grades 8 through 12. Since 2001, there has been a 130% increase in the number of international students attending the school. Over 56 languages are spoken in the student population. Van Tech offers a full slate of academic courses plus 12 specialized programs designed for students with unique needs. The staff consists of 100 teachers and 35 support staff. The site of Vancouver Technical Secondary School covers 20 acres and includes several buildings covering 30,000 square meters. It is located on Vancouver's east side and is the largest inner-city school in the district.

David Derpak became the principal of Van Tech in the fall of 2002. As part of his preparation, David met with the student council and a number of staff members to begin learning about the school. He was told that there were concerns about student conduct and attendance, as well as vandalism and graffiti. He was also told that some staff members were reluctant to go into the hallways between classes. Students identified safety and spitting in the school as their main concerns.

Getting Started

David began by working with his vice principals, Gino Bondi and Hank Lyth, to establish a shared vision of the school culture they wanted to create. While they agreed that student achievement and ongoing staff development were of paramount importance, they realized that until issues of vandalism, graffiti, and student deportment were addressed, it would be hard to focus on the high expectations they held for student and staff achievement. There was a strong desire to establish an academic tone *in* the school and a safety zone *around* the school. As an administrative team, they committed to doing whatever it took to create a school environment in which all students and staff could feel safe. They began to collect and analyze information about current vandalism, graffiti, tardiness, absences, and discipline issues. At the same time, they talked with students about the importance of attendance, punctuality, and appropriate behavior. Teachers began to start their classes on time, regardless of whether all students were there, as a means of reinforcing punctuality. Regular announcements over the intercom reminded students to be punctual and requested that staff step out into the hallways to assist the students.

At the same time, the administrative team, along with the police officer assigned to the school, focused on being highly visible by being out in the hallways before and between classes. Their primary purpose was to assist with hallway conduct and to encourage students to get to classes on time. It was also their aim to make positive connections and build relationships with the students. Visibility at Vancouver Technical Secondary School is no small challenge, even with a team of five people. Beginning on the first day of school, the team selected a different hallway for each class change throughout the day, and they never missed a class break for the first 3 months of the year. The team carried walkie-talkies to facilitate communication. They were careful not to establish a predictable pattern for where they would appear at breaks. Students soon began to comment that they felt like the team was everywhere.

Van Tech is very old, built in 1927, with underground tunnels connecting the various buildings. Members of the team might be speaking to students in one hall and then use a tunnel to show up in another hall without ever having been seen moving through the building! With the adults in the school being so highly visible, student behavior, punctuality, and attendance improved dramatically almost immediately. Vandalism and graffiti rates plummeted, and a safe and orderly tone was established.

Student deportment at assemblies was another area targeted by the team. They were explicit about their expectations for appropriate behavior: removing hats, sitting with feet on the floor, listening respectfully to speakers, and responding appropriately to what was being said. The administrative team was diligent in reinforcing these guidelines. As a result, students quickly learned that inappropriate behavior during assembly would not go unnoticed.

While extremely effective, this approach was not without its ramifications. Even positive change to an existing culture disturbs the equilibrium of the school and is not likely to be entirely understood or trusted at first. The administrative team began to hear from students and parents that their actions were being viewed as militaristic and too authoritarian. This was a signal for them to regroup and approach things differently. They did not abandon their commitment to improving the school climate, but they did take things more slowly for a period of time during which they continued to talk with students and parents about why they were so determined to improve attendance, punctuality, the appearance of the school, and student deportment.

Staff supported the appointment of a climate department head whose responsibilities would be to focus on school climate, conditions for high achievement, social responsibility, and student conduct. Working with the climate department head, students conducted a schoolwide survey to learn about personal safety concerns being felt by students. The survey showed that bullying and harassment were on the minds of most students, especially those in the younger grades. Their response was to establish a program called BASE (Building a Safer Environment). BASE is a mentoring program that connects senior students with eighth-grade students to support them as they make the transition to their new school.

Current data pertaining to what the Van Tech staff calls *Social Responsibility* indicate vast improvement in a number of areas:

- Over a 4-year period, costs for repairing vandalism in the school have been reduced from more than $22,000 a year to less than $8,500. The staff are proud of the fact that their interior graffiti bill for the 2005–06 year was only $84.97 and that window damage dropped to $4,000 from over $14,000.

- In the 3 school years from 2002–03 to 2004–05, overall attendance saw an improvement of 41% in absences and 43% in tardiness. The greatest improvement was an increase in attendance from 80% to 92% within the First Nations population.

- In the same 3-year period, there has been a 40% reduction in suspensions and a 61% reduction in administration-initiated student transfers.

Commitment to a shared vision coupled with a willingness to adapt and consider alternative points of view yielded positive outcomes for the collaborative efforts of the Van Tech administrative team. By the end of the 2004–05 school year, David and the staff of Van Tech were satisfied that the environment of their school had improved sufficiently. The role of climate department head could, therefore, be discontinued.

High Expectations for Student Success

As the previous section illustrates, high expectations for student deportment are clearly communicated and actively supported at Vancouver Technical. High expectations also exist for student academic achievement, regardless of ability or program level. In a school the size of Vancouver Technical, there are many stories of high standards held and the collaborative work done by staff to ensure that students meet them. While there are too many to recount here, the following examples will serve to highlight some of them.

Grade-Level Meetings. Grade-level meetings are held formally once a month and informally once a week. They are attended by the grade-level counselor, the vice principal responsible for that grade, and the First Nations support worker. The purpose of these meetings is to identify students at all points on the learning spectrum who are exhibiting a need for additional support. Interventions are tailored to address the needs of those students. Sometimes the support focuses on assistance with organization, sometimes counseling intervention is required, and at other times specialized instruction is the answer. The goal of the grade-level meetings is early identification and intervention so that all students, regardless of skill level, can meet with success. There are many stories of student success as a result of the support and intervention developed in the grade-level meetings. It is significant to note that 65% of Van Tech First Nations students graduate. Provincial and city graduation rates for First Nations students are 31% and 51%, respectively.

Honor Roll Assemblies. A student honor roll is established for each grading period to honor students who maintain a 3.125 (about 83%) grade average. Once the names are assembled, students are invited to an assembly at which their accomplishments are celebrated with applause, snacks, and hot chocolate or ice-cream sundaes, depending upon the weather! This practice serves to recognize those who are doing good work and provides an incentive to those who would benefit from working harder. Currently about 44% of each class has achieved honor-roll status.

Scholarship Group. The staff at Van Tech is diligent in their efforts to address the needs of students who struggle. They are equally diligent about addressing the needs of top achievers. Using final exam results from the

High Expectations Lead to Success

- Van Tech students received 40% of the Duke of Edinburgh Gold awards.

- Van Tech students raise the most funds for Variety Awards of all BC schools.

- Provincial exam marks exceed the average for all public schools in English 12, French 12, Français Langue 12, and Geology 12.

previous year, plus first-term report cards and teacher recommendations, approximately 40 high-achieving grade 12 students are identified each year to become part of what is called the *Scholarship Group*. Using the same criteria, 10 of the top achievers in grade 11 are also invited to join the group. In addition, each of the 11 feeder schools is asked to identify two grade 7 students to become involved in the Scholarship Group. The inclusion of students who will be entering Van Tech the following year sets the stage for the years ahead by communicating high expectations and demonstrating support for academic achievement.

Letters containing current research on learning are sent to the identified students, and sessions are organized to assist them with such things as study habits, improving letter grades, goal-setting, memorization, and stress management. The scholarship program supplements the work being done by classroom teachers by providing strategies for meeting academic challenges and information about scholarships that exist and how to earn them.

Scholarships Earned by Percent of Graduating Class

2002	22 (6.5%)
2003	30 (9.5%)
2004	31 (9.7%)
2005	33 (12.9%)
2006	36 (11%)
2007	30 (10.3%)

A Van Tech Story About High Expectations and Success

In 2001, Van Tech student involvement in science fairs was nonexistent. The teachers in the science department were concerned that students were missing out on authentic learning about scientific inquiry and research methods, as well as organization and project completion. Through collegial discussion, they decided to require that all students in grades 8, 9, and 10, as well as senior biology students, complete a science fair project as part of their course requirements on an annual basis. This practice has yielded exceptional results. Students begin in grade 8 with rudimentary understanding of the scientific process and method; over the years, their skill level and confidence as learners develop to the point that by later grades, they are doing original research and dealing with complex issues.

The staff realized at the outset that its largest challenge would be parental support, because many parents do not speak English, nor do many of them have an educational level that allows them to support their kids in sophisticated, scientific research for these projects. To compensate, teachers in the science department spend countless hours in class and after school assisting students. A university mentorship program was also established, which allows students to access university labs where practicing scientists assist them with their projects. With these supports in place, all students complete a science fair project every year.

The Vancouver Technical science fair program is now one of the strongest science fair programs in Canada, with approximately 600 projects involving more than 1,000 students involved annually. Van Tech students consistently receive recognition and awards at the regional and national levels. In 2007, four Van Tech students were selected to join Team BC and attend the Canada-wide science fair in Nova Scotia. All four students won awards. In addition, two grade 12 students received cash awards and were offered entrance scholarships by the University of British Columbia, Dalhousie University, and the University of Western Ontario as a result of their science fair projects.

In the words of the science department head, Clive Jibodh, and Regional Science Fair chair and Van Tech science teacher, Devon Ross, the success of the science fair "is due to the incredible work ethic of students, along with the dedication of an entire department to make a difference in our students' lives."

High Expectations for Staff Learning and Professional Involvement

The science fair initiative is just one example of the many collaborative processes in place at Vancouver Technical. Other examples include the following:

- In a collaborative model for school decision-making, all deliberations are vetted through an elected staff committee that includes one administrator. The staff committee reaches out to the rest of the staff for input and feedback.

- Teachers collaborate on a school finance committee to allocate the school budget.

- An interview committee involves teachers working with administrators to interview new staff.

- The School Planning Council includes teachers, students, support staff, and parents. It monitors the school growth plan and examines all school resources, including staff and fund allocations.

- Teachers regularly work in teams of a variety of configurations to analyze and use data to plan instruction as well as to address student needs. The staff has designed a system they call *collab time* in an effort to expand their opportunities to meet with each other and with students in specialized groupings. Collab time occurs eight times over the course of a year. On collab days, the start time for students is moved back to 10:15 a.m. to provide time for the meetings. Teachers spend some of the collab time meeting in departments and some of it meeting in other group configurations to focus on instructional strategies.

Looking Back With Satisfaction

David Derpak is passionate about his work at Vancouver Technical Secondary School. He loves to come to work and thrives on the energy and challenges inherent in a school the size of Van Tech. He says that the staff is wonderful. David is of the opinion that this staff could be placed in any school and significant improvement would follow. Perhaps the most telling evidence of the effectiveness of the work being done at Van Tech is reflected in the words of the president of the Grad 2007 Committee, who said that "the teachers at Vancouver Technical are more like friends than teachers. They care about the kids, watch out for them, and treat them like people, not just students." She went on to say that "kids want to be at school, and they want to do well to meet their teachers' expectations."

Khowhemun Elementary School

Khowhemun Elementary School is located in Duncan, British Columbia, a small city on Vancouver Island with a population of 77,000. It is a kindergarten to grade 6 school with a steady enrollment of 350 students. Students come from middle- and low-income families as well as from families that receive income assistance. In recent years, the First Nations population from both on and off reserve has risen from 30% to 50%. The number of students with special needs has also increased. Transience is a significant issue at Khowhemun.

The British Columbia Ministry of Education creates school profiles to provide information about BC schools. The profile provides information about individual schools as well as provincial data for comparison. Table 6-1 contains demographic information from the Khowhemun school profile.

Table 6-1: School Profile for Khowhemun Elementary School

	Khowhemun	Province
Families with annual income below $30,000	30%	23%
Single parent families	30%	16%
Parents who graduated from high school	66%	76%
Parent(s) with postsecondary degrees	10%	18%

The University of British Columbia's Early Childhood Development Mapping Project identified Khowhemun as one of three schools in Duncan with the neediest populations. A high proportion of students and families were identified as vulnerable in a significant number of subcategories, including the following:

- Readiness for school

- Language and cognitive development

- Physical health and well-being

- Socioeconomic factors (for example, family income)

In 2001, when Charlie Coleman became the principal at Khowhemun, his vision was for the school to become what he calls a *results-based learning community*. He started by analyzing the data at hand with a view to taking a clear and honest look at what was happening at the school. He found that for many years, Khowhemun had been a 70/30 school—one in which 70% of the students met expectations and 30% did not. Charlie's first step toward developing the results-based learning community that he envisioned was to present these and other findings to the staff. Charlie and the staff decided that being a 70/30 school was not acceptable. Together, they committed to improving student achievement results. They agreed that they would have to do that by improving learning conditions and professional practice.

There are really two phases to Charlie's work with the Khowhemun staff: the first 3 years and the years following.

The First Three Years

During the first 3 years, the major focus was on reading. A number of structural and instructional approaches were taken that were quite global in nature.

Structural changes to the timetable and support systems took this form:

- Recess was moved to the afternoon to allow for an uninterrupted academic focus in the morning.

- The timetable was constructed to provide blocks of what was referred to as *sacred time* for reading instruction.

- Improved attendance and punctuality were supported through the efforts of the Aboriginal Support Worker and Healthy Schools Intervention Worker.

- Learning Assistance time was increased, and additional support teacher time was provided in support of uninterrupted reading instruction.

- English as a Second Dialect time was increased and targeted for oral language support.

- School-based professional development focused on school goals in the areas of literacy, numeracy, and social responsibility.

Instructional adaptations included:

- Use of British Columbia Performance Standards for planning and assessment in the areas of reading and numeracy

- Guided reading within a balanced reading program at the primary grades

- The use of Reading 44, a K–10 classroom reading program developed by British Columbia teachers in North Vancouver, as a core framework for collaboration and planning around reading instruction

- Strategies such as buddy reading, read-a-thons, celebrity readers, reading clubs, and accelerated reader and home reading kits to promote and enhance the joy of reading

- Regular visits to the public library, with every student getting a library card

- Targeted interventions for struggling readers

- Small-group work to support such things as oral language development, guided reading, and literature circles

From the Balcony

The staff at Khowhemun is extremely hard-working and very caring. During the first 3 years, they worked diligently to provide the conditions that would ensure improved school and student success. Over time, however, their enthusiasm and commitment were put to the test in a variety of ways. In addition to the challenges presented by the high-needs population they served, there were two significant in-school barriers that had an impact on the climate at Khowhemun School. The first was the fact that class composition was becoming increasingly complex, with the arrival of more and more students with multifaceted needs. For 3 consecutive years, the school saw walk-in registrations each September of approximately 60 students, the vast majority of whom arrived working below grade level. This influx was disruptive for start-up and planning. It was also discouraging because most of the new arrivals proved to be transient. These factors, coupled with decreasing levels of funded support staff, made it progressively more difficult to sustain the momentum for improvement that had been built. The stresses of the classroom brought about by the challenges of their high-needs population and decreasing levels of support combined to have a negative impact on the staff's ability to sustain the work they had begun. In Charlie's words, "We feared we had hit a plateau both in terms of results and staff energy toward these efforts. We recognized that if we kept doing the same things, we should not expect different results."

Together, Charlie and the staff acknowledged that as a learning community, they would need to find ways to adapt strategies and practices to address their changed reality. A leadership team consisting of administration and representatives of classroom and specialist teachers was created. Together, that group successfully pursued a 2-year action research grant from the Society for the Advancement of Excellence in Education (SAEE). The mission of SAEE is to develop new Canadian knowledge on school improvement and foster the understanding of its use. The society supports public schools and those who work with them to improve outcomes for all students. With the grant came outside researchers to assist their school improvement efforts, as well as funding to facilitate their work. A researcher from SAEE plus a research partner from the local Malaspina University-College (now called Vancouver Island University) provided expertise for the staff as they planned their research.

The funds helped the staff to acquire learning resources for students and teachers. They were also used to provide release time to facilitate action research, through which classroom teachers tried new instructional strategies, with a view to gauging their effectiveness based on student progress. The grant money also supported professional development through action research. It is important to note that funds were not used to hire additional staff; instead, the decision was made to concentrate on learning and new practices that could be sustained long past the availability of grant funding. The grant from SAEE helped the staff of Khowhemun to refocus their efforts and renew their energy.

Onward and Ever Upward!

Having received the SAEE grant, the staff of Khowhemun redoubled their efforts to identify promising practices that fit the needs of their students. They focused on differentiated learning approaches, including—but not limited to—multiple intelligences and learning styles. Their work was done within the context of an action-research model at all grade levels to answer the question, How will the use of teaching strategies focused on the multiple intelligences of our students measurably improve reading success for all students, especially our most "at risk" and "vulnerable" students?

The stated objectives for the action research being done at Khowhemun were as follows:

1. Enhance reading instruction, intervention, and enrichment for all students.

2. Increase use of teaching strategies that match students' multiple intelligences and learning styles.

3. Track individual student progress and adapt for individual needs.

The work done in the years before receiving the SAEE grant provided a strong foundation upon which to build. The explicit focus on individualization and differentiation through multiple intelligences led to more precise learning and intervention in a number of areas. Classroom teachers at Khowhemun took risks and collectively learned from both successes and mistakes.

Reading Support Groups. A Reading Support Group Team was formed to organize and provide small-group reading support to every student in every grade four times per week. Depending upon the nature of the group activity, students are grouped according to reading level, learning style, or multiple intelligences. There is no learning assistance stigma attached to reading group time because all students participate. It is a normal part of instructional practice at Khowhemun. Because the groups are flexible, depending upon the focus, membership in them changes periodically. This has been the most popular and positive outcome of the action research project. In the safety of small groups, students have taken learning risks, and teachers have tried new instructional strategies. In the reading groups, students and teachers learned together. Both took their learning back to the classroom, so there was spillover into other areas.

Organizational Structures. A number of critical organizational practices supported the action research being done at Khowhemun:

- **Keeping reading time sacred**—Nothing was allowed to interfere with the Reading Support Group schedule.

- **Making teacher learning a priority**

  ◊ School-based in-service time was provided regularly to allow staff to learn and plan new strategies together.

  ◊ Grade groups met to compare their action research strategies and results.

  ◊ The whole staff met regularly to share their work.

- **Using measurement results to inform instruction**

  ◊ The transient nature of the school population resulted in significant demographic changes, making trends year over year difficult to compare.

◊ To more accurately gauge the impact of the work they were doing, the staff of Khowhemun tracked the progress of all students on an individual basis using common assessment tools for pre- and post-assessment. Instruction was designed based on assessment results.

◊ Critical achievement data were collected for students at risk. This allowed the staff to target intervention more effectively.

◊ Individual assessments were used in conjunction with schoolwide data.

Professional Learning. All staff at Khowhemun adopted a learning stance in their work. Their involvement in action research and focus on multiple intelligence and learning style theory provided a common framework within which to collaborate.

• School-based in-service sessions allowed staff to work collaboratively to identify high-yield strategies from multiple intelligence and learning styles research for instruction, intervention, and enrichment. Professional resources were purchased and studied to assist with this work.

• Grade-level team teachers each selected one or two specific strategies on which to do individual action research.

• Teams shared the outcomes of their action research with the rest of the staff at staff meetings, in-services, and team meetings.

• Some staff attended conferences and returned to the school to share what they had learned with their colleagues.

Shared Leadership. The Lead Team, which was instrumental in securing the SAEE grant, has taken a proactive leadership role and has collaborated closely with the external research partners from SAEE and Vancouver Island University. Members of the team have coordinated the small reading groups, tracked individual student progress, and collaborated with staff to use the information in their work with students. In addition, some members from the Lead Team have initiated grade-group sharing sessions and related professional development. The work of the Lead Team has provided support and impetus for leadership to be distributed throughout the staff. As teachers have worked together to conduct action research and share their learning with each other, they have all shared instructional leadership responsibilities.

Outcomes. The British Columbia Performance Standards describe and illustrate four levels of student performance, ranging from not yet within expectations to exceeding expectations in standards relevant to reading, writing, numeracy, social responsibility, and technology. Beginning in 2002, the staff at Khowhemun used these performance standards to gauge student achievement in reading and mathematics each term. For the first 3 years, they saw consistent growth; however, they observed that the changing demographics and increased transience rates that began in 2004 had an impact on the overall scores. Figures 6-1 and 6-2 illustrate longitudinal scores in mathematics and reading over a 4-year period. This information, along with the shift they were experiencing in the student population, led the staff of Khowhemun to conclude that they were no longer getting the critical evidence they needed to have an impact on the scores of individual students. They began to consider other ways to use data in their work.

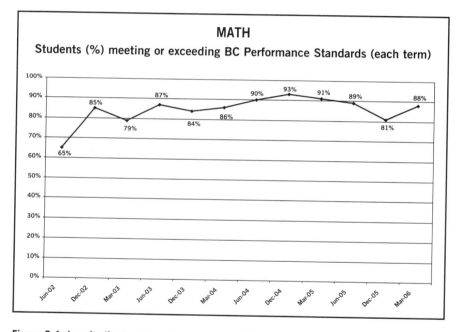

Figure 6-1: Longitudinal mathematics scores on BC performance standards

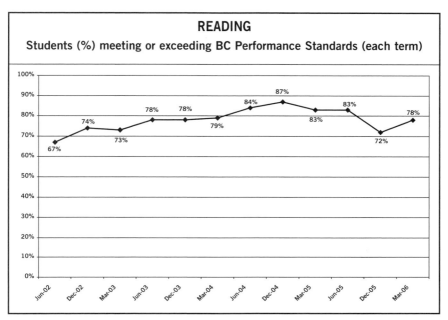

Figure 6-2: Longitudinal reading scores on BC performance standards

As part of their action research initiative, the staff decided to take a more precise approach to their work with students who were not yet within expectations. In September 2005, they started to *individually* track a cohort of 86 students who were at risk. Over a 2-year period, the number of students dropped to 54 due to transience and to students moving on to middle school. The staff is satisfied that using this approach, nobody falls through the cracks!

- Twenty-eight students improved by two grade levels or more (52%).

  ◊ Of these 28 students, 13 were Aboriginal.

- Seventeen students improved by one grade level or more (31%).

  ◊ Of these 17 students, 12 were Aboriginal.

- Nine students showed minimal growth (16%).

  ◊ Of these nine students, five were Aboriginal.

  ◊ Eight of these nine students have either been identified as learning disabled or are awaiting assessment.

- All students have Individualized Education Plans (IEPs).

Looking Back With Satisfaction

While the SAEE funding has ended, the good work that it facilitated has continued, albeit in a less formal way. In Charlie's words:

> While we are very happy with the measurable and anecdotal results to date, we recognize that this is a work-in-progress. A professional learning community must always be willing to learn, grow, and change. An action research team must be willing to adjust and adapt based on the results of the research. This is energy-consuming work, but the rewards have been great. Becoming an effective learning community requires that professional commitment and personal relationships are strong. To confront the data and attempt new strategies there must be trust and mutual respect. We will continue this work-in-progress, always with a focus on student learning.

Charlie Coleman transferred to Quamichan Middle School in September 2007, where he is facing new challenges and working to build a strong results-focused learning community in his new school. The staff of Khowhemun will miss his leadership, but there is little doubt that their focus on learning—both their students' and their own—will continue.

Sir John A. Macdonald Secondary School

Sir John A. Macdonald Secondary School (SJAM), with a population of 1,330, is located in Hamilton, Ontario. Canadian-born students, including a sizeable group of Aboriginal students, study alongside ESL students coming from about 80 countries and speaking more than 50 languages. Aboriginal, in this context, refers to First Nations, Métis, and Inuit people. Many of the students (502) were born outside of Canada, and other than English, the primary languages spoken in the school are Vietnamese, Afghani (Pashto), and Somali. There are 84 teachers and 23 support staff working with students from grades 9 through 12.

Michael Rehill wears two hats in his professional life. He is the principal of Sir John A. Macdonald Secondary School as well as of SHAE, an Aboriginal alternative education school. SHAE stands for Strengthening Hamilton Aboriginal Education. He is very proud of the school, saying that it "exudes excellence in academics, sports, clubs, activities, and community involvement." Michael asserts that "the ability to achieve excellence is possible because of our dedicated students and committed staff, who are continually challenging themselves to be the best they can be." Staff and students have high expectations for themselves and for each other.

In a school as large and diverse as SJAM, there are many examples of teachers working collaboratively to achieve excellence in program and instruction. One initiative stands out as being a particularly unique form of collaboration that has yielded exceptional results for a population of Aboriginal students at risk.

NYAWEH: The Aboriginal Stay-in-School Initiative

In 2003, studies focusing on Aboriginal youth in Hamilton revealed that the high school dropout rate was alarming. At that time, the city had a reported Aboriginal population of 12,000, and only 48% had high school diplomas. The research concluded that the dropout rate could be attributed to a number of factors, including poor health, lack of academic success, and poor socioeconomic conditions. Aboriginal youth surveyed during the study indicated that due to the lack of culturally relevant curriculum and culturally sensitive support, they were not interested in school.

The Stay-in-School Initiative was established with the goal of offering the supports necessary for Aboriginal students to successfully attain an Ontario Secondary School Diploma. It was implemented in two downtown Hamilton schools: Sir John A. Macdonald Secondary School (public) and Cathedral High School (Catholic) in September 2003 and January 2004, respectively. The students named the program NYAWEH, the acronym for Native Youth Advancement With Education Hamilton. It is also the Mohawk word for *thank you.*

A Unique Collaboration Between School and Community. Originally funded by the Hamilton Community Foundation Young Family Response Fund, the program is now in its second phase. NYAWEH is a collaborative venture between the Hamilton-Wentworth District School Board (HWDSB), the Hamilton-Wentworth Catholic District School Board (HWCDSB), and the Hamilton Executive Directors' Aboriginal Coalition (HEDAC). The program is advised and resourced by the Hamilton Aboriginal Education Council (HAEC), which is chaired by Taunya Laslo, the executive director of the lead agency—the Niwasa Head Start Aboriginal Preschool.

Members of the Hamilton Aboriginal Education Council

Chair of Niwasa Head Start Aboriginal Preschool—NYAWEH sponsoring agency

HWDSB administration

HWCDSB administration

Principals of the two schools

Elders

Aboriginal youth advisors

Hamilton Community Foundation

Parent and youth representatives

Representatives from each of the Aboriginal agencies in Hamilton

The final project report for the 2003–2006 phase of the Aboriginal Stay-in-School Initiative states the mission statement for this unique collaborative venture as follows:

> The NYAWEH Program endeavors to provide a support system based on Aboriginal culture and academia that allows Aboriginal students to flourish within Hamilton's Secondary School environment.
>
> NYAWEH cultivates the relationship between the culture of First Nations people and mainstream education. Both forms of education are integral to the progress of Aboriginal youth and are viewed as necessary assets in building healthy individuals, communities and nations.

(Aboriginal Stay-in-School Initiative, 2006)

A Unique Opportunity for Aboriginal Youth. The NYAWEH program is housed in a dedicated resource room with a youth advisor available for consultation and advocacy regarding cultural, academic, and economic issues facing Aboriginal students in the school system. The room contains computers with Internet access, a comprehensive library with resources containing culturally based content, school supplies, and nutritional snacks and meals. Students utilize the room to complete assignments, get tutoring help, seek cultural support and guidance, and resolve peer or teacher conflicts.

A cultural outreach worker also visits community schools to present cultural education programs and help Aboriginal students to self-identify in order to receive support or participate in Aboriginal programs. This worker also mentors NYAWEH students in their traditional teachings and works to develop Native Studies classes.

Indicators of NYAWEH Success at Sir John A. Macdonald Secondary School.

- When the program first began in September 2003, there were four youth enrolled in the program at Sir John A. Macdonald. At the end of 3 years, the enrollment had grown to 90. As of 2007, when it was into its second phase, the NYAWEH Macdonald program served 80 students.

- NYAWEH sustains an average retention rate of 75%.

- The credit accumulation rate of Aboriginal students who participate in NYAWEH is significantly higher than those who do not (see Figure 6-3, page 120).

- The suspension rate has dropped significantly (see Figure 6-4, page 120).

- Seventeen NYAWEH and SHAE students have graduated.

- Course offerings specific to Aboriginal culture are offered in visual arts, history, and social science.

- Two youth drum groups have been formed, and they perform extensively for a variety of events throughout Hamilton and Southern Ontario. The boys call themselves *Young Spirit* and the girls call themselves *Sweetgrass Sisters*.

- The Aboriginal community has been mobilized through the formation of HAEC, and they have provided input into the district's Aboriginal Education 5-year plan.

- The Aboriginal self-identification policy has been accepted.

- The program youth workers are able to manage the program with minimal outside support.

- NYAWEH and SHAE provide a continuum of education for disengaged Aboriginal youth in alternative education programs. The youth worker at SHAE works with the NYAWEH youth workers to provide cultural support as students make the transition into Macdonald and Cathedral High Schools.

- The NYAWEH program is now in Phase 2. Clearly the unique collaboration between school and community has been successful.

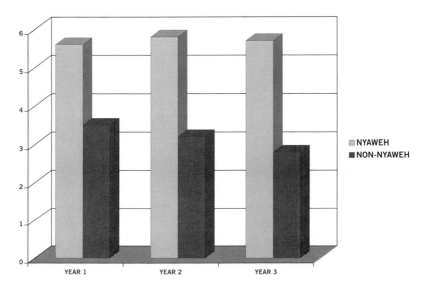

Figure 6-3: Credit accumulation of Aboriginal students at SJAM

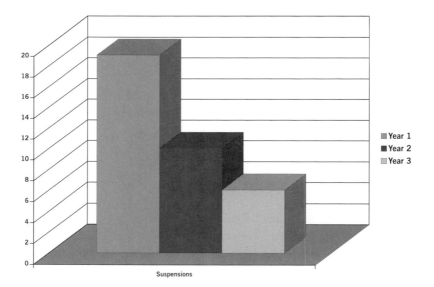

Figure 6-4: Suspensions of SJAM NYAWEH students

Lessons Learned Through This Unique Collaborative Venture. The final report for the first phase of NYAWEH cites numerous lessons learned as a result of the work done between 2003 and 2006. The program partners recognized, upon reflection, that the importance of many of these lessons had either been underestimated or unanticipated when they first began to collaborate on the project. The lessons learned conclude that, in order for a program such as this to thrive, there must be:

- Champions within the school, the school system, and the community

- A common vision

- A dedicated program space

- An environment in which diversity already flourishes

- Constant advocacy for the youth and the program

- A professional learning community within the school that can connect students to the supports they need

- Public education related to issues facing urban Aboriginal people

- Mentors within the project to motivate and educate the staff members who are working directly with the students

- Realistic timelines allocated to deliver objectives while building capacity

- Willingness for stakeholders to take healthy risks and think creatively

- A strong reporting and communication strategy

- A comprehensive data-tracking and analysis system

- Opportunities to celebrate student and program success

- Relevance of all aspects of the program to urban Aboriginal youth

- Budget consideration given to things like nutrition, transportation, extracurricular trips, and support for life necessities for the students

Looking Back With Satisfaction

The personal stories told by the students who participate in NYAWEH bear testimony to the impact of this program. Daily, students tell the youth advisors, "If it weren't for this program, I wouldn't be here." These students, who have struggled with challenges that normally keep them alienated from the education system, have made a choice to partner with NYAWEH because it is often the only place they can feel safe and welcome. Through NYAWEH they receive supports that are essential for their survival as well as for success in life.

A vision shared by stakeholders from many different places, combined with moral purpose and commitment to making a difference for Aboriginal youth, resulted in the creation of a program that makes a difference to all of the students within it. This unique collaboration between school and community partners has offered Hamilton's Aboriginal youth an opportunity to invest in their future through the NYAWEH program.

Summary

Striving to address the diverse student needs being experienced in today's schools presents educators with myriad challenges that are unique to each school environment. It is possible to address those issues, but not without a pervasive attitude among the staff that makes it acceptable to try as many times as necessary to find the solutions. Solutions to adaptive challenges do not readily present themselves, and more often than not, the first attempt at solving them will fall short. A staff working in an environment that is safe and orderly, and in a culture of high expectations for themselves and their students, will do whatever it takes to ensure success for all. Chapter 7 focuses on the recognition that a climate of high expectations for success means that growth and learning for all must be continually moving forward. Attention to time on task and opportunity to learn are required to facilitate continuous growth and learning for both students and staff.

Getting It Right Once Is Not Enough . . . Growth and Learning Must Be Ongoing

Teaching is never static. It is a people business and as a result is never predictable—and never boring! Our profession is continually evolving as we discover more and more about the learning process. The world, too, is constantly changing; all of which serves to make the teaching profession both complex and exciting.

In chapter 6, the point was made that theories and research findings provide important guidance for schools; however, because each school's culture is unique, these findings are not universally applicable. The reality is that theories evolve. What is current today will become passé before long, as new research reveals fresh insights and knowledge. Educators need to make sense of new knowledge through thought, discussion, and shared learning.

Professional growth and learning are not options. Professional people working in a culture of learning that is truly collaborative and responsive to new information accept that what worked in one context may not necessarily work in another. The complexity of our work, along with a rapidly changing world, make our chances for getting it right over the long term almost impossible if we simply repeatedly do the same things. Successful professional practice is predicated on reflection about what is currently working and what is not. Flexibility, shared learning, and ongoing growth are the markers of successful learning communities inhabited by educators who are committed to continuous learning and collaborative work to identify and address the learning needs of all students.

Schools that are continually getting better keep student learning central to the work they do. Providing students with adequate time on task and opportunity to learn is a priority to ensure that they can meet high expectations for success. Just as students must be provided with adequate time on task and opportunities to learn, so too must the adults who support them. In fact, educators are the most significant learners in a school community because their deliberation, ongoing growth, and professional intervention will serve the learning needs of students, parents, and other supporting adults.

The Link to Effective Schools Research

Synergy between the correlates results in effective schools. Improvement efforts that are guided by the correlates are most likely to result in sustainable success. To this point, we have seen the power of a clear and focused mission that is accompanied by strong instructional leadership at the school level. We have also seen the impact of frequent monitoring of student progress on achievement and know that high expectations for success within a safe and orderly environment are prerequisite to making learning by all a reality.

> In schools that are Harbors of Hope, learning by all is a reality. In these schools, the correlates work in concert and are interdependent. All seven are consistently present and powerfully demonstrated.

High expectations that are realistic and achievable must be accompanied by strong, effective supports to ensure success. Lezotte and McKee (2002) stated the importance of teachers having a "clear understanding of essential learner objectives, grade-by-grade and subject-by-subject" (p. 21). They also said that once there is clarity in terms of what students should be learning, they must be given adequate time and opportunity to do so. Lezotte and McKee spoke of the "zone of proximal development," which they defined as "the relative distance the new learning can be from prior learning before the learner can and will be able to successfully learn the new material"(p. 160). Simply stated, if students have already mastered the material being taught, they may become bored and disengaged. By the same token, students who lack the prior knowledge or skills required to be successful may become discouraged and give up. In both cases, the students involved are being denied the opportunity to learn.

Accordingly, teacher learning should focus on identifying essential curricular learnings, assessing to ascertain current skill and knowledge levels, and planning instruction in a way that will guarantee optimal student time on task and opportunity to learn.

What We Have Learned About the Lesson

Ongoing staff development is mandatory to ensure well-defined pedagogical skills and current knowledge about high-yield strategies for learning. Life in schools is incredibly busy, and it is easy to get lost in the routine day-to-day business of teaching and dealing with students. Unless teachers and school systems make explicit efforts to make quality professional development a priority, it may get lost in the shuffle.

There are many different ways to pursue professional development, and all have merit, depending upon the purpose of the learning. Attendance at conferences and workshops, taking courses, participating in mentorship programs, and attending study groups are just some of the forums for teacher learning. On-the-job or school-based training is now recognized as the method of staff development that is most likely to result in sustained overall school improvement. Job-embedded staff development is hands-on and requires that teachers engage in their learning through working collaboratively with colleagues on school-based issues. When teachers create knowledge and engage in action research together, everybody learns from each other—and the students benefit. Learning by all becomes a reality.

Working in professional learning teams, teachers have the opportunity to reflect on issues pertaining directly to their work with students. They will spot the areas in which they need information and training. The teams can identify topics on which to focus whole-school professional development, as well as individual professional growth, and can make plans to address both. This shared instructional leadership will ensure that professional development initiatives are pertinent, that sufficient time for collaboration is built into the school day, and that needed resources are made available to support teacher learning. Adequate time on task and opportunity to learn are as critical for educators as for students. In fact, without adequate time and opportunity to pursue their own professional learning, teachers are hard pressed to ensure that the same conditions are provided for their students.

Ensuring Success

Effective schools work on the premise that learning is nonnegotiable and that time and support for the learning to occur must be variable and responsive to student needs. Many schools think in terms of a pyramid of interventions that provides time and support to students who are struggling academically. We believe, however, that learning goes beyond academics. To be effective in addressing all aspects of student learning, we must adjust our thinking to include social, emotional, and personal learning as well.

The Battle River School Division in Camrose, Alberta has developed a "Pyramid of Success" that guides their work with students (see Figure 7-1). It shows three levels of intervention to address all aspects of learning. *Proactive* intervention occurs in the classroom as a result of ongoing monitoring and effective formative assessment to identify problems early and provide assistance as soon as students show evidence of difficulty. *Responsive* intervention, the next level, indicates that teachers must be responsive to students whose needs go further than what can be effectively addressed by proactive classroom practice. This level of support may require a different instructional approach and draw upon school resources beyond the classroom. For students who need even more specialized support, *individualized* interventions may utilize services beyond the school. To be effective, these three levels of intervention must reside in a culture that values relationships and character as highly as academic achievement. In such a system, students can be given time to learn and opportunity for overall individual success, whether through varying instructional approaches, one-to-one support, small group work, or specialized programming.

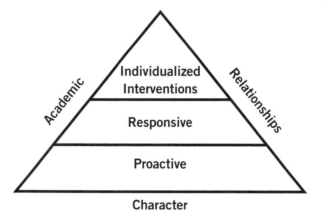

Figure 7-1: The Battle River School Division's Pyramid of Success

Planning Time on Task and Opportunity to Learn

Schmoker (2006) declared that "the single greatest determinant of learning is not socioeconomic factors or funding levels. It is instruction" (p. 7). Instruction must be focused to ensure that students are learning at the highest possible level. The only way to make certain that learning is occurring is to regularly check for understanding.

Fisher and Frey (2007) maintained that students come to learning experiences with varied background knowledge that influences how they will understand new material. Unless teachers regularly check for understanding, it is difficult to know what they are getting from the instruction. Often students think they understand, but when it comes time to demonstrate what they know and can do, they stumble. Other students think they understand, but have some interfering misconceptions. Checking for understanding is the purpose for formative assessment, which, if used well, helps teachers to improve their instruction and students to monitor their own progress.

Like Lezotte and McKee (2002), Fullan, Hill, and Crevola (2006) stressed the importance of "ensuring that students are operating in their zone of proximal development, where competence and challenge are aligned. . . . For students to make significant learning gains, instruction must be focused on meeting the needs of the individuals within the classroom" and not merely following the prescribed curriculum or program (p. 64). They advocated for precision teaching for every student based on measurement and feedback. In precision teaching, "hallmark" teachers operate in a "focused instructional mode consistently on a day-to-day basis for all students" (p. 66).

Effective assessment provides information on student instructional needs as well as an early warning for students needing direct intervention. Based on what assessment tells teachers about learning needs, students can be grouped and regrouped as necessary to provide focused teaching that is targeted to address identified needs. Fullan, Hill, and Crevola (2006) also stressed the importance of the effective use of small instructional groups and a variety of instructional strategies to promote focused learning. They cautioned us to remember that "narrowing the achievement gap and providing equal opportunities for all students is not the same as providing equal time to all students. Some students need more time and more support" (p. 76). They advocated for daily, short, and focused small-group instruction times for students who struggle, in order to improve their chances for success.

Providing Time and Opportunity for Students Who Struggle

Differentiated instructional practice and flexibility are the solutions to providing students with the time they need to learn and an opportunity for success. Practicing differentiated instruction does not mean teaching everything in a myriad of ways; rather, it means matching instruction to the needs of each learner. Carolan and Guinn (2007) identified four characteristics that are common to classrooms typified by differentiated practice:

1. They offer personalized scaffolding. Scaffolds are temporary supports that help to bridge the gap between what learners presently know and can do and what they are learning. Awareness of student progress and the ability to provide timely intervention when they falter provide a scaffold to keep them moving forward. Scaffolding support can be provided through individualized assistance and the use of learning crutches like metaphors, rhythm, acronyms, and other tailored supports to enhance learning opportunities.

2. They use flexible means to reach defined ends. Clear learning goals and an understanding of related skills and knowledge provide the foundation for instruction. Offering multiple ways for students to learn and demonstrate what they know and can do is one of the hallmarks of successful differentiation.

3. They mine subject-area expertise. Effective teachers not only know their subject matter, they also know what students require in order to understand it, what preconceptions they might have, what is likely to cause students to struggle, and how to accommodate different student strengths and learning styles in their instruction.

4. They create caring classrooms. Differentiated instruction is really about honoring diversity and creating a respectful classroom environment in which students understand that people learn in different ways.

Guskey (2007, p. 29) spoke of the need to use a structured classroom corrective process to help students "use formative assessment results to improve their mastery of the concepts and skills" they are working on. Students need "alternative pathways to learning success, adapted to meet their individual learning needs and interests" (p. 29). Effective corrective processes have three essential characteristics that make student engagement in the instruction significantly different from the initial learning activity:

1. They present the concepts differently. Format, organization, or method of presentation is changed.

2. They engage students differently in the learning. Different learning styles or forms of multiple intelligence are addressed.

3. They provide students with successful learning experiences that leave students better prepared, more confident, and more motivated for future learning.

Types of Corrective Activities

- Reteaching

- Individual tutoring

- Peer tutoring

- Cooperative teams

- Textbooks

- Alternative textbooks

- Alternative materials, workbooks, and study guides

- Academic games

- Learning kits

- Learning centers and laboratories

- Computer activities

Working With Resistant Students

Providing time on task and opportunity to learn for students who struggle academically presents one set of challenges. Doing the same for students who appear unwilling to learn is a different story. Students who present as resistant are usually students who feel hopeless and helpless. Their despair might originate from home or from school—or from both. While circumstances beyond the school are difficult to address, school personnel can design school-based solutions to work with students who are disengaged.

Darling-Hammond and Ifill-Lynch (2006) suggested that the creation of a "strong, academic culture that changes students' beliefs and behaviors, convincing them to engage with their school work," is critical to working with students who resist for whatever reason (p. 9).

They offer numerous suggestions for creating space and time for homework. In their opinion, schools need to "make it harder not to do the work than to do it!" (p. 12). Options that have been successful in this regard include:

- Using block scheduling and double periods to extend learning time

- Adding homework time

  ◊ At the beginning or end of the day

  ◊ During advisory periods to provide adult support

  ◊ At Saturday sessions

  ◊ At weekday breakfast clubs

  ◊ During after-school programs run by community organizations

  ◊ In any setting that provides dedicated time and personalization

- Creating a "success class" that takes place during elective periods and focuses on skill-building and work completion

- Establishing daily drop-in periods voluntarily supervised by teachers who simply provide an opportunity for students to work in the presence of a caring, supportive adult

Commitment to providing time on task and opportunity to learn requires that time and support be viewed as expandable. Resistant students may require extra time to complete work, or they may need an opportunity to finish incomplete work. To do this, staff members must share a common vision of what it means to truly support struggling learners and what structures must exist to make the vision a reality.

Creating a Strong Academic Culture

- Assign work that is worthy of effort.

- Make the work doable.

- Find out what students need.

- Create space and time for homework.

- Make learning targets and desired quality public and explicit.

- Collaborate—it is the key.

What the Lesson Teaches Us

- What is current in education today rapidly becomes passé as new research reveals fresh insights and knowledge.

- Ongoing professional growth and development are not optional.

- Improving schools are inhabited by educators who are committed to continuous learning.

- School-based on-the-job training is most effective for sustaining overall school improvement.

- Once there is clarity in terms of what needs to be learned, adequate time and opportunity to do so must be provided.

- Just as students must be provided with adequate time on task and opportunities to learn, the adults who support them must also have time and opportunity to learn.

- Teachers must identify essential learnings and then assess current skill and knowledge levels in order to determine what each student requires in terms of time and opportunity.

- When students work in their zone of proximal development, competence and challenge are aligned.

- The only way to ensure that learning is occurring is to use formative assessment strategies regularly to check for understanding.

- Effective formative assessment provides information on instructional needs as well as an early warning system when students start to falter.

- Learning is nonnegotiable; time on task and opportunity to learn are.

- A pyramid of success ensures that required interventions are proactive, responsive, and individualized within a culture that values academics, relationships, and character.

- Some students need more time and support than others.

- Differentiated instruction means matching instruction, time, and support to the needs of each learner.

- Successful differentiation offers scaffolds and multiple ways for students to demonstrate what they know and can do.

- While teacher knowledge of content is critical, it is equally important that they have an understanding of student learning needs and knowledge of how to meet them.

- Differentiated instruction honors diversity and promotes comfort with taking the risks required to learn.

- Effective corrective activities and instructional strategies provide students with alternative pathways to learning success.

- Students who are resistant or disengaged are most often those who feel hopeless and helpless.

- A strong academic culture, along with tangible supports for success, can improve student attitude, attendance, and behavior.

- Tangible supports are those that make it harder *not* to do the work than to do it.

- The creation of a strong academic culture requires that staff share a vision about what it takes to support struggling learners.

Lessons Lived: Stories From the Real World

To be truly effective, schools must adopt an attitude toward school and student success characterized by commitment to ongoing improvement. The three schools featured here illustrate the many positive outcomes that result from a planning process that celebrates success as well as accepts the requirement for continuous learning and professional growth.

Carlton Comprehensive High School

Carlton Comprehensive High School is located in Saskatchewan. It is the largest high school in the province with over 2,000 students in grades 9 through 12. There are three satellite schools and 139.25 fulltime equivalent staff positions consisting of both teaching and nonteaching staff. The administrative team consists of Dawn Kilmer, the principal, and three vice principals.

The student population is drawn from a large geographical region of the province that includes the city of Prince Albert. Approximately 5% of the students come from northern Saskatchewan communities; 52% have declared Aboriginal ancestry.

Carlton is a uniquely equipped facility with a swimming pool, large auditorium, three gymnasiums, many computer labs, and a state-of-the-art library. Students enjoy tennis courts, an all-weather track, soccer pitches, football fields, softball and baseball diamonds, and access to an ice surface for rink sports. As a comprehensive high school, Carlton offers over 170 courses in the academic, fine arts, vocational, and trades areas. Many of the teachers in the trades areas are journeymen, thus enabling students to begin their apprenticeship training while still in high school. Carlton offers a wide range of club and cocurricular opportunities as well.

Making It Work in a Large Setting

A school as large and diverse as Carlton cannot be effective unless structures for effective communication are established and staff members work collaboratively based on common values. At Carlton, the values are clearly stated and easily recognized. The staff is passionate about learning for all . . . whatever it takes. In the words of a Carlton staff member, "If we envision it and it's better for kids, we will make it happen."

The Carlton staff works in a variety of PLC team contexts to share information about student achievement, discuss instruction, and plan to meet student needs. One of the teachers states that working in a PLC team allows staff to share experience and learn from one another "so that we can create the best learning environment for our students. We are doing this to maximize student learning." Another teacher says, "We trust each other so we can take risks, then share." As a result of their collaborative efforts, the approach in all disciplines has shifted from "I teach. You learn" to, "Have you learned? If not, let's try this approach."

This attitude has resulted in Carlton teachers working creatively and with persistence to find ways to help all students achieve success in the regular classroom setting and through a broad range of other programs and supports. Modified classes no longer exist, except in mathematics. In all other disciplines, students requiring program modification are integrated into the regular classroom, where teachers differentiate instruction for them according to their learning needs and styles. These instructional adaptations have made it possible for more students to achieve regular credits, and the number of modified credits granted has been reduced significantly.

Attendance Desk is an in-house computerized student record system developed by one of the Carlton staff that has proven very efficient and versatile. As needs are identified, the program is altered to make additional functions available. Attendance Desk has significantly simplified gathering data about student achievement. One feature, for example, allows teachers to keep track of instructional adaptations that have proven effective for individual students. This highly valued feature saves instruction time by allowing teachers to get information about specific student needs early each semester. It also serves as a database for teachers to search for ideas about adaptations that have been used effectively by other teachers.

Teacher Leaders (department heads) meet regularly with the administrative team to share information about students and explore issues. They share the discussion with others in the department to gather their input, which is then taken back to the administrative team. This communication loop ensures that when items come to the full staff, no one is surprised. Staff members feel they have had a chance to influence the outcome to meet their common goal of doing what is best for the school and students.

Learning for All . . . Whatever It Takes

From the time they enter grade 9, Carlton students are supported in becoming independent and thinking seriously about what they want to do when they leave school. Staff members encourage long-term planning, what they refer to as "dreaming the big dream." Students are given opportunities to research what it will take to bring their dreams to fruition. School counselors work with students from grades 9 and 10 to help them understand course requirements and prerequisites for postsecondary endeavors. Over time, this approach has resulted in fewer timetable changes. At the end of the 2006–07 school year, students graduated with an average of 28 credits, compared with an average of 26 credits 3 years earlier. With encouragement and assistance, students set goals and keep their options open.

At Carlton, grades are not a clear indicator of where students are in terms of graduation. A number of students have social and emotional life issues that result in having to either reduce their school involvement or leave and return later. Such issues might include teenage pregnancy, alcohol and other drug addictions, and sexual or physical abuse. In response to this, the Carlton staff has designed a variety of locations and programs that allow multiple re-entry points or, in many instances, re-entry at any time. This has stopped the loss of students because they know that changes in program delivery and location can be arranged, and they know that they can begin again when they are ready. In Dawn's words, "We are continually striving for success for *all* students. We are a flexible school that is big on learning!" In describing how staff members work, Dawn states that if things are not working for a student, they will work on finding a plan B—or C—or whatever works. The staff prides itself on the transition and retransition opportunities they provide, and they work hard at maximizing success for all.

For the most part, the only students who leave the school are those who transfer out. Students are rarely asked to leave. If students stop attending, one of the counselors or educational associates will contact them to find a way to keep them involved. Fueled by their commitment to provide time on task and opportunity to learn, the staff of Carlton Comprehensive High School has certainly done what it takes to provide a full slate of opportunities for students to be successful both within and beyond the regular classroom:

- The extension campus serves students ages 16–21 with varying needs, including those who are upgrading to get to University and those who, for whatever reason, are unable to continue in the regular classroom. Time restraints have been removed from this area. Once a student completes a module of work, it is marked and kept until the student is 22 years old. Twenty-nine courses are offered through the extension campus.

- The Learning Assistance Center (LAC) offers a variety of services including tutorial assistance, exam support (such as oral testing, scribing, and so on), and consultative support for teachers working with students with diverse learning needs and styles or with PPPs (Personal Program Plans). In addition, staff of the LAC offer formal and informal assessments and learning skills assistance. The LAC collaborates with the extension campus to support students who have difficulty completing or are unsuccessful in their regular courses. With LAC support, students can rescue credit by working on the units they did not complete successfully in the regular classroom setting.

- Summer school is offered the first 3 weeks of July so that students can retake or get ahead on courses of concern to them. If students are retaking a course, their previous teacher provides information to focus learning on the parts of the curriculum they need the most help with. Summer school at Carlton boasts an 85% success rate. Classes are also made available to people over the age of 22 who are no longer on the school register. Using extension campus materials, they are able to take summer-school courses at any time throughout the year.

- Outdoor School focuses on environmental education. It occurs for the most part in an outdoor setting and focuses on developing understanding, appreciation, and use of natural resources. Students enrolled in the outdoor school earn credits in language arts, mathematics, geography, work experience, biology, and physical education over the course of a full semester. This program adopts the practices of *Out to Learn: Guidelines and Standards for Outdoor Environmental Education,* created by Saskatchewan Education, and enjoys a 100% success rate.

- Won-Ska Cultural School, one of Carlton's satellite schools, is committed to working with the community to transition Aboriginal students back into the school or to helping them get an education in some form. Students can enter Won-Ska at any time.

- Learners With Purpose (LWP), another satellite school, makes it possible for students to continue their education when they cannot attend Carlton (for any reason). In the 2006–07 school year, four students graduated from high school through this program. Students can enter LWP at any time during the year.

- The Northgate Program offers the regular curriculum in a block setting to students at risk in grades 10, 11, and 12 who would benefit from closer supervision and early intervention when attitudes and behaviors start to interfere with their success. There are four entry points during the year.

- The Opportunity for Success room was created to address the needs of students at risk who have the ability to be successful, but have not done well in the regular classroom. These students are typically 18 years of age or older and just cannot operate in the regular classroom. They often have learning disabilities and/or social or behavior problems that interfere with their ability to handle quick transitions and the pace of the regular classroom. They need the consistency and individualized instruction that can be provided in the Opportunity for Success room. On average, this room serves 10 students, although the numbers sometimes increase. Students can enter this room at any time.

- Two transitions classes exist for students who are 16 years old but have not yet attained a grade 9 standing. These classes focus on basic skills in literacy and numeracy. Students can enter transition classes quarterly.

- The Work Transitions program, for students at risk aged 17–19, focuses on the skills required for work placement and includes job placements during the school year. The program does not emphasize credits; instead, a job coach works with students on employability skills.

- An alternate education program provides an opportunity for students who have not seen success in regular programming in spite of adaptations and extra supports. This program focuses on classroom-based preparation for the workforce for 50% of the time and has students in work placements for the other 50% of the time. Over 290 business partners provide learning opportunities for Carlton students in work settings. These courses last a year, and students can enter at any time.

- Life skills and developmental education programs exist for those students with very complex needs on individualized programs. Entry times are flexible; however, due to the complexity of student needs, enrollment is limited to 12 students in each class.

Looking Back With Satisfaction

The Carlton staff functions as a team. They see themselves and each other as leaders. In their words, "We're always in the process of renewal. Together, we force ourselves into actualization of the curriculum." One teacher writes:

I feel very lucky to be part of the Carlton community. In both the social sciences and math departments we are encouraged to share materials, discuss student achievement, and standardize our expectations in the classroom. Not only do we do this on an informal level amongst colleagues, we are also allotted time during professional development days and allowed to free up time during the day to observe other teachers and plan collaboratively.

Another teacher says that Carlton has become the school it is as a result of teachers being allowed to "grow with a vision and a dream that they believe will improve student outcomes." Still another teacher states, "We're a 30-year work in progress." That may be so; however, in the interim, it is clear that if the staff envisions something that will be better for their students, they will find a way to make it happen.

Committed educators who share a passion and a vision for making a difference for all of their students, the impressive administration and staff of Carlton Comprehensive High have found many ways to provide all students with adequate time on task and the opportunity to be successful.

École Charleswood School

Located in Winnipeg, Manitoba, École Charleswood School has a population of 450 students in grades 7–9, with a small international student and declared Aboriginal component. All socioeconomic levels are represented in the school.

École Charleswood School is a dual-track setting that offers English instruction to students in grades 7–9 and French Immersion to grades 7 and 8. Grade 9 French Immersion students attend a nearby high school. Of the 55 staff members, 40 are teachers and 15 are teaching assistants. Charleswood straddles two educational program levels in Manitoba; grades 7 and 8 are considered middle years, while grade 9 is considered a senior year and operates on the credit system.

Creating a Climate to Support Learning for All . . . Whatever It Takes

When Iain Riffel assumed the role of principal in September 2003, he and the vice principal, Patt Roberts, began to talk with the staff immediately about working together to create and sustain a climate that would support learning for all. Guided by effective schools research, the Charleswood staff rewrote their mission statement as follows:

Together we motivate students to succeed in academics, athletics and the arts by the opportunities we offer and the relationships we build.

Expectations for students and staff are clearly stated:

We expect our kids to be good students, be good friends and neighbours, and to admit and fix their mistakes. We work with students so that they are known for being thoughtful and responsible in their academic work, in the quality of their character and in citizenship.

At Charleswood, we, the staff, hope to . . .

- Keep our students on-board.

- Promote mutual respect and student/staff cohesion.

- Respond to students who struggle and to those who don't behave.

- Maintain a positive staff culture and healthy outlook.

- Promote staff support and togetherness.

- Strengthen classroom practice, expand cross-grade school-wide opportunities and keep our professional development relevant.

- Maintain our building with pride.

- Be mindful of our wellness, comfort and safety.

Having articulated expectations, the staff went on to identify successful behaviors (see Table 7-1). They included parents in this thinking as well to ensure that all stakeholders understood their roles in making their stated mission meaningful and relevant.

Table 7-1: Qualities of Successful Charleswood Students, Parents, and Staff

Successful Students	Parents of Students Who Are Successful	Parents of Students Who Struggle	Effective Staff
• Regularly attend class on time. • Arrive prepared for class (with their books in hand). • Meet deadlines (with assignments done on time and projects done over time instead of at the last minute). • Study for tests (with regular review, study notes, and so on). • Behave (by listening to teachers and being helpful). • Show kindness to others. • Get involved in other aspects of the school (sports, clubs, student council). • Connect with positive peer influence. • Regularly connect with a trusted adult in the school. • Talk with their parents about school.	• Establish a home environment that supports children as students and connects student learning to outside opportunities. • Communicate regularly with the school. • Volunteer and are regularly present at the school. • Follow additional learning suggestions from the school. • Are involved in school decision-making.	• Schedule and structure homework. • Review student agendas and homework for completion and quality. • Provide direct help and/or supervision. • Support the teachers at the school. • Call the teacher(s) and school when in doubt.	• Share a mission, vision, and values. • Collaborate on essential curricular outcomes, instructional strategies, common assessments, results analyses, and interventions for students who don't learn. • Inquire about best practice in light of the current reality. • Experiment, act, and analyze results (reflect). • Commit to continuous improvement. • Make time to nurture personal relationships and professional ties. • Remember to support each other and help each other bounce back in times of need.

> ## Effective Schools
>
> 1. Focus on indicators of attitude, attendance, behavior, and achievement.
> 2. Have a safe and orderly environment, a clear and focused mission, a climate of high expectations for success, shared instructional leadership, and opportunities to learn.
> 3. Monitor student progress and establish regular home-school partnerships.
> 4. Have a climate and culture that support individual and collective growth.
> 5. Provide for extra time and support to students who don't learn.
> 6. Provide for extra time and support for teacher teams to collaborate.

The staff went on to express their vision of the effective school they would work to create at École Charleswood School.

How Do They Walk the Talk? The staff at Charleswood walks its talk in four ways, explicitly focusing on 1) data; 2) improving student literacy levels; 3) enhancing the learning environment; and 4) creating classroom-based and schoolwide structures to support students.

An Explicit Focus on Data. Charleswood focuses on gathering, understanding, and using critical evidence to create collective wisdom that guides short-term planning and future directions in the areas of achievement, attendance, attitude, and behavior. Measurement results are organized to provide both schoolwide and grade-level specific information. Schoolwide data are used to inform school planning in the spring. Grade-level data are used mid-year, when teachers and support staff meet to identify and plan for students deemed to be at risk, and during transition meetings held in the fall.

Initially, Iain took responsibility for the collection of data and created what he calls "data packs" to focus staff discussion and planning in the areas of achievement, behavior, attendance, and attitude—the four key indicators of school effectiveness. The contents of a data pack are shown in Table 7-2. Over time, the staff realized the value of the data and began to ask for more specific grade-level data to meet their needs. Many are now tracking their own data and using measurements to determine whether goals have been met.

An Explicit Focus on Improving Student Literacy Levels. The staff at Charleswood identified a need to focus on improving student literacy levels and has made this a priority since 2003. Using the Dysanti Close test, students entering grade 7 are assessed for decoding and fluency. Students achieving

Table 7-2: Data Pack Contents

Schoolwide Measurement			
Achievement	**Behavior**	**Attendance**	**Attitude**
Term-end mark reports • Honors • At risk • Failure • Senior 1 (grade 9) missed compulsory credit	Tracking Form Summary provides information about referrals for administrative intervention with students.	Term-end summary	Divisional survey results • Students • Parents • Staff
Awards Report summarizes annual information on how many students achieved honor-roll status in each grade; how many were acknowledged for participation in cocurricular activities, and how many have been recognized more than once.	Class Removal Lists Summary provides information about students who are sent to the office and why they were sent.		
Learning Assistance Support (Resource)			
Literacy • Library usage • Library circulation			

below grade level are pulled out of regular classes into an intensive daily reading program for a 6-to-8-week period, either in small homogeneous groups or individually. In-class adjustments are made to accommodate the students involved in the daily reading program. Members of the Support Services Team run the program, review progress periodically, and share information with classroom teachers and parents. After 6 to 8 weeks, students either continue in or leave the program (with commitment to periodic check-ins to monitor their progress). All students are again assessed in September of their eighth-grade year for transition purposes and to verify the effectiveness of interventions already in place.

Support Services Team members have been afforded many professional development opportunities and have pursued coursework in literacy and reading. Literacy and reading in the content areas are also a PD focus for many classroom teachers. The professional growth plans of many teachers also focus on support strategies for struggling students. Staff development in all of these areas is a priority at Charleswood.

An Explicit Focus on Enhancing the Learning Environment. The school library was made a central focus for literacy development and was reconceptualized to offer services beyond the traditional library services. The Centre Médiathèque is staffed by a Learning Resource teacher who focuses specifically on improving the literacy of students in the school. Services include assessing literacy levels, operating book clubs, and providing guest speakers, as well as integrating technology and training. The Centre is also a hub for staff development topics such as literature circles and literacy-building strategies across the curriculum. The number of books in the center per student doubled between the 2003–04 and the 2006–07 school years. In the same period, the number of student visits per month to the library outside of regular school hours increased by 25–50% depending upon the month, and the number of books in circulation increased on average by 15%. Between 2003 and 2006, the school underwent many renovations in classroom and specialty areas as well. Classrooms contain new materials, and access to technology has been enhanced. The staff has been involved in planning for the renovations as well as the purchase of equipment and materials.

An Explicit Focus on Creating Classroom-Based and Schoolwide Structures to Support Students. A wide variety of supports and interventions are in place to respond to the needs of students at Charleswood:

- The Student Services Team meets with the school administration and grade-level teams every cycle to review literacy and numeracy assessment data, discuss student progress, reflect on the efficacy of the schoolwide supports for meeting the diverse needs of struggling students, and adjust system responses as required.

- The Resource Room staff members assist students with exam preparation, test writing, assignment or project completion, study skills, organization, and tutoring. The Resource Room also provides respite and emotional support for students when needed. Tutoring services on a drop-in or appointment basis are available at lunch and before and after school. During the school day, some students have regularly scheduled time in the Resource Room, and teachers refer others as necessary.

- The Classroom Alternative Room provides long-term placement for students who are predisposed to social difficulties and experience problems with learning in the regular classroom setting. Most often, students are referred to the alternative program by classroom teachers, support staff, or administration, but occasionally students and their parents self-refer. Student involvement in the alternative program is part of a larger plan for success which includes divisional psychologists and social workers collaborating with school staff and parents in support of the students. Students participate in developing their plan for success, and involvement in the alternative program is offered as a voluntary option. Review meetings are held with parents of students in the program every 6 weeks.

The nature of the program varies from year to year, based on the needs of the students who are enrolled. While some students receive their entire core academic subjects in the Classroom Alternative Room, others attend for just part of each day. The program enhances life skills through exposure to work experience and wellness opportunities and accommodates flexible entry and exit times. Students make the transition back into the regular program as they are able to.

- Grade 9 students can opt out of one elective credit in order to receive extra time and help on their compulsory courses through the Resource Room.

- Dedicated SOK (Save Our Kids) periods allow teachers to focus on core course learning objectives with students at risk. Each subject area receives approximately three periods per 6-day cycle to devote to SOK activities. The teachers plan the activities, how they will deliver them, and which students will be involved. They work with students either individually or in small groups on such things as organization; study strategies; goal-setting, reflection, and celebrating interviews; and subject-area support (catch up and review). The Student Services Team is instrumental in implementing, facilitating, and evaluating the impact of this level of support for students.

Looking Back With Satisfaction

In reflecting upon the work done by the staff at École Charleswood School, Iain states that data alone "does not capture the essence, ownership, and chemistry that exemplify the fine work of staff and students. There is much work and progress that cannot be typified in numbers." He goes on to say, "At Charleswood, the greatest collaboration is exercised between staff in planning around individual kids. Everyone is willing to do something.

Someone is always willing to step up and engender a positive and deep relationship with identified students with the hope of making a difference."

In September 2008, Iain assumed the principalship of Shaftesbury High School. In his time at Charleswood, he and the staff created a solid foundation upon which to build.

Harry Sayers Elementary School

Susan Antak has been the principal of Harry Sayers Elementary School (HSES) since 2002. Located in Abbotsford, British Columbia, Harry Sayers has a population of 460 K–5 students. There are 26.8 fulltime equivalent teachers and five teaching assistants on staff. Other teaching supports include part-time services of a counselor, a speech pathologist, a multicultural worker, and a vice principal, who also serves as librarian and writer of individualized education plans.

Harry Sayers is an exceptional school in that 98% of the school population is comprised of new Canadians. Most of the children enrolled in kindergarten were born in Canada, while their parents were born in India or Pakistan. Language and cultural differences have prompted school and district staff to learn about the cultural norms of the families in their community in order to respond with the understanding and sensitivity necessary to develop effective working relationships.

Punjabi is the language spoken in most homes; there are few strong English-language role models for students entering kindergarten. Many of them speak little or no English, and few have had the benefit of a preschool experience. Some students are missing the oral language experiences that are necessary for language growth and as a result are also not proficient in their home language. Approximately 70% of the students at Harry Sayers are designated ESL students, and most receive support from kindergarten to grade 4. Language barriers have a significant impact on student progress toward meeting academic expectations outlined by provincial standards.

Many parents in the community are not familiar with the Canadian school system and do not understand the expectations for achievement at all grade levels. They are generally supportive of school programs, but communication is difficult. Parents need support to understand the home-school partnerships that facilitate student growth. It is common for families to remove children from school for up to 4 months to take extended vacations back to India and Pakistan. Staff members are working with parents to encourage them to plan their vacations around the natural breaks in the school year, because extended absences have a significant detrimental effect on student academic growth.

Building Bridges With the Parent Community

The staff at Harry Sayers has made a concerted effort to involve parents in the life of the school. To facilitate communication, translators are available, as required, for meetings and conferences. In addition, student planners provide school information in both English and Punjabi. Parents are invited to attend weekly assemblies that reinforce behavioral expectations, the school's "Reach for the Stars" motto, and the virtue of the week. Assemblies focus on individual and classroom accomplishments and upcoming school events.

REACH for the Stars
Respect
Effort
Attitude
Cooperation
Honesty

While parents support school initiatives, they are reluctant to volunteer for school or district committees. Personal invitations have been issued to parents to work with staff on the parent advisory council and the school planning council. Babysitting service is provided to facilitate their attendance at these meetings. In June 2003, the staff collaborated with parents to help them reach their goal of implementing a school uniform dress code. A parent survey, which had an 84% return rate, showed that 92% of parents responding favored the adoption of a school uniform dress code. The dress code was implemented in January 2004.

The staff at Harry Sayers has reached out successfully to the parent community to build bridges of communication and collaboration. The result has been learning for all. Staff members have had much to learn about their clientele; parents have had much to learn about how to support their children at school; and students have had much to learn about Canadian culture and the English language. Susan and the staff at Harry Sayers have done a remarkable job of making time to learn and opportunities for success available for all involved: students, staff, and parents.

Time to Learn and Opportunities for Success . . . for Students

Harry Sayers students are meeting numeracy expectations at all levels; however, literacy achievement falls below district targets. As a result, the 2007–08 School Plan for Student Success focuses on improving reading comprehension and oral communication for students at all grade levels. The staff has been explicit in identifying time, resources, and organizational structures to support work in those areas. Learning objectives and instructional strategies have been identified for all grade levels, and common assessment tools are used to measure progress.

Time

- Timetables are organized to provide uninterrupted blocks of time for literacy instruction for K–5 students in all classes.

- Computer lab timetables are organized so that classes at all levels can use educational software twice each week from SuccessMaker reading and spelling programs.

- Time is scheduled each day in all classes to DEAR (Drop Everything and Read) for 20–30 minutes.

- Teachers collaborate to set weekly times for students to meet for buddy reading programs that pair reluctant readers in grades 3–5 with K–2 students for reading activities for at least 30 minutes per week. This experience provides opportunities for older readers to experience success as they read to their younger buddies, and younger students benefit from the modeling provided by their older buddies.

- The school's library program schedules story time for children from the onsite preschool programs.

Resources

- The school has acquired a wide variety of professional resources pertaining to assessment and instruction to support literacy instruction, along with leveled books and dual language books to facilitate appropriate choices for students' independent reading. The Kiwanis Club "Read Around the World" program has supported the creation of classroom libraries at all levels. In addition, the staff has developed home reading programs.

Organization

- Instruction includes three guided-reading lessons a week.

- Teaching assistants support learners at risk in classroom literacy programs.

- ESL instruction provides three levels of support to students: those with high needs meet three times per week, those with moderate needs twice a week, and those with low needs once a week.

- Students at risk receive extended literacy instruction twice weekly.

- Students from a neighboring high school earn credits by coming to Harry Sayers to provide literacy support for the younger students.

Strategies to Improve Student Performance

- Time
- Support
  ◊ Resources
  ◊ Organizational structures

Time to Learn and Opportunities for Success . . . for Teachers

The staff at Harry Sayers have worked diligently to learn about their school community and acquire the knowledge and skills they need to work with them to support student growth effectively. In Susan's words, "A good school keeps looking at itself, questioning its operation, and making adjustments accordingly." With clear and aligned goals in the areas of reading comprehension and oral communication, staff members have learned with and from each other to become increasingly proficient in their work. They have also accessed the support of district specialists and learned from outside experts. Staff development at Harry Sayers Elementary is both focused and multifaceted:

- Each grade has a teacher representative who meets with administrators to establish objectives for grade meetings and coordinate staff meeting discussions.

- Teachers work in grade-level PLC teams to align curricula, review targets, and examine student progress. They also collaborate to select resources, attend workshops, and share best practices with each other.

- In their pursuit of optimal learning experiences for students, teachers often participate in pilot projects that allow them to try out new resources, programs, and assessment instruments.

- A diverse group of teachers and specialist staff from all grades meets monthly to share insights on professional reading materials related to the school literacy goals.

- Professional development days allocated to the school are dedicated to reading comprehension and oral communication.

- Portions of biweekly staff meetings are dedicated to sharing best practices in literacy and oral communication with colleagues.

- Lunch 'n Literacy sessions are scheduled throughout the year for teachers to view videos, share practices, and hold miniworkshops pertaining to literacy and oral communication.

- During the 2006–07 school year, staff participated as partners in the ESL in the Mainstream project. This involved 12 2-hour training sessions as well as grade-level group meetings to collaborate on project objectives, language goals, curriculum objectives, project assignments, and related activities that teachers tried out between sessions. The whole-staff focus on ESL in the Mainstream provided rich opportunities for powerful discussion and collaborative work.

Time to Learn and Opportunities for Success . . . for Parents

The staff has made a concerted effort to encourage and facilitate the parent community becoming involved with the school:

- A district multicultural worker is available to meet with parents 1 half-day each week.

- Miniworkshops are provided at parent advisory council meetings on topics such as home-school partnerships, home support for reading and writing, homework and study skills, report cards and how to interpret them, health and nutrition, and how to become involved in your child's school.

- Newsletters provide tips on ways parents can assist their children with developing reading, writing, and math skills.

- Handouts are developed for parents about how to support their children's learning.

- The Parents as Literacy Supporters (PALS) program is available for kindergarten and grade 1 students and their parents. PALS is a commercial program that the staff has adapted to help them support parents in their efforts to work with their children at home. Parents of kindergarten students join their children in the classroom for 1 hour per month to be part of lessons that focus on topics such as learning the alphabet, early math development, learning to write, and reading with children. A translator is provided for each session. Grade 1 teachers also hold PALS sessions throughout the year.

- The school library purchases bilingual books and holds drop-in library sessions for preschool children and their caregivers twice each month. The staff model—in English and Punjabi—how to involve children while reading a story to them.

- Programs are established in partnership with the school district, Abbotsford Community Services, Family Centre, the City of Abbotsford, and the University College of the Fraser Valley to provide opportunities for parents and children in the community.

  ◊ Neighborhood Place is housed in a portable classroom affiliated with Harry Sayers. The service provider for Neighborhood Place is Family Centre. Neighborhood Place offers a variety of programs for preschoolers and caregivers.

    + ABC-123 is a structured preschool program for children 3–5 years of age. This half-hour program, which is held twice weekly, focuses on building literacy skills, preparing children for school, and improving social skills through play and learning. ABC-123 helps parents make sense of the Canadian school system while offering support, friendship, services, and information to families and caregivers. Additional services include Toddler Time (0–3 years), Community Drop-In (0–5 years), Stay 'n' Play Drop-In (0–5 years), Meet and Greet Drop-In (0–5 years), and Pajamarama Story Time (0–5 years).

  ◊ The Ready, Set, Learn Program is a provincial initiative for preschoolers that annually supports schools as they present a series of Ready, Set, Learn events for parents and their 3- and 4-year-olds. The goal of the program is to promote positive connections with the school system and raise awareness of community agencies that can provide helpful resources, support, and information.

◊ The PACT (Parents and Children Together) program is a partnership between the school, the University College of the Fraser Valley, and Abbotsford Community Services. Beginning in January 2008, the PACT initiative includes a weekly parenting program focusing on parenting skills and English literacy on Friday afternoons. The program provides babysitting and is free to parents and caregivers with children who are 3–5 years of age.

Looking Back With Satisfaction

In March 2005, the work done by the staff at Harry Sayers Elementary School to address the needs of all members of their school community was acknowledged when they received the Fraser Valley Cultural Diversity Award for Inclusive Environment. The award recognized the school for providing a welcoming environment for all students, parents, and people in their neighborhood.

Susan and the staff of Harry Sayers have faced many unique challenges in their work. They have been creative and resourceful, striking supportive partnerships with many external agencies, and are always focused on social, emotional, and academic success for students. Time to learn and opportunities for success have been provided to all members of the community, and the results have been gratifying.

Summary

Our work as educators is never dull. To work effectively with our students, we must understand them as learners and do whatever it takes to accommodate the many, varied influences that affect their ability to succeed. We must commit to ongoing growth and professional learning. We must be flexible and creative, tenacious in our efforts to provide time and opportunity to support learning by all teachers, students, and parents.

Academic learning is only one aspect of the learning that occurs in schools. Social, emotional, and personal learning must also be a focus. Chapter 8 deals with the umbrella curriculum and the "soft skills" that students must acquire if they are to be adequately prepared for the future into which they will graduate.

Academics Are the Focus . . .
But Other Things Matter, Too

Academics must be a priority for schools; however, to genuinely address the whole child, learning must go beyond the formal curricula that are among the tools of our profession. When we consider the rate at which the world is changing and becoming smaller through advances in science and technology, we must acknowledge that the world into which today's children and youth will graduate is vastly different than it was even 10 years ago. Globalization of economies is resulting in increased international trade. It is imperative that cultural differences be respected and language barriers overcome to respond to the changes we are dealing with today and the challenges we are likely to face in the future. Health and security issues are pressing and must be dealt with on an international level if successful solutions are to be found.

Changing demographics are having an enormous impact on schools. According to the 2006 census done by Statistics Canada, more than half of all Aboriginal people in Canada are under the age of 25 (Statistics Canada, 2008). In addition, an increasing number of new immigrants creates a diversity in schools that mimics the diversity of the world. As a society and as educators, we must respond to the unique needs of all students by identifying and actively teaching the skills and attitudes they will need in the future.

Our educational mandate must shift toward preparing students to become citizens of the world. To do this will require a concerted effort on the part of all educational stakeholders as well as parents and the broader community. School personnel must make it a goal to forge positive relationships with the parents and caregivers wherever possible. It is also important to establish productive relationships with members of the community at large. Through collaborative working relationships with parents and the community, schools can enhance their ability to help students prepare for life in the adult world.

The Link to Effective Schools Research

The prominent correlate in this lesson is "Positive home-school relations." While it is possible for schools to meet student needs effectively without a great deal of parent/caregiver support or involvement, it is much easier if the other significant adults in students' lives are also involved. Forging relationships with families is complicated by factors such as transience, job demands on parent time, poverty, and language barriers. Many parents have not had positive school experiences themselves, and they may be reluctant to engage with their children's teachers. In any case, it is important that schools make a genuine effort to invite parental involvement and, where necessary, facilitate it by helping families understand the school, its goals, and its practices. With support and encouragement, all parents can contribute to the school and their children's education.

By the same token, teachers receive little, if any, preparation in their training for establishing collaborative partnerships with parents. As a result, contact with parents often provokes anxiety and apprehension in teachers who may fear the worst, especially if they have unhappy news to share. Lezotte and McKee (2002) maintained that "teachers need training and support on how to deal with a wide variety of parenting styles" and that school administrators must be "prepared to support the teachers in their efforts to make such partnerships work on behalf of all students" (p. 163).

> In schools that are Harbors of Hope, learning by all is a reality. In these schools, the correlates work in concert and are interdependent. All seven are consistently present and powerfully demonstrated.

The effective schools continuous improvement system is based on the belief that all students can and will learn, regardless of their family background. In an ideal world, parents and teachers will form a partnership in support of students. When the ideal is not possible, we must find other alternatives. Lezotte and McKee supported the creation of academic foster programs that could involve senior citizens or other members of the community as mentors to students whose parents are inaccessible, either through disinterest or circumstance.

There may be a number of people in the community who would value the opportunity to contribute by working directly with children. With appropriate support and monitoring, these people can provide invaluable service and assistance for all children, especially those who are at risk. Members of the community are not always able to directly engage with school activities, but they may be able to help schools by providing services or monetary support. Positive home-school-community relations are critical to the work that schools must do to prepare all students for the future.

What We Have Learned About the Lesson

Mel Levine (2007) referred to students leaving the school system as "start-up adults" and identified what he called "soft skills," the presence or absence of which will have an impact on their success regardless of their postsecondary pursuits.

Soft Skills

Levine identified the soft skills as interpretation, instrumentation, interaction, and inner direction, and asserted that they are the "gear" that students needed to have in their "cognitive backpacks" to be fully prepared for adulthood (p. 17).

Interpretation

Students skilled in the soft skill of interpretation:

- Recognize that the ability to memorize is not sufficient for true comprehension.

- Are able to use higher order thinking skills such as analysis, compare and contrast, synthesis, evaluation, and judgment.

- Have strong metacognitive understanding about how to learn in order to pursue and make sense of new knowledge.

- Are able to draw upon prior knowledge and experience to engage mentally.

In Levine's words, "a vibrant mind vibrates" (2007, p. 19).

Instrumentation

Students skilled in the soft skill of instrumentation:

- Have a project mentality, exhibited in their ability to set goals and bring them to fruition through effective time management and prioritization.

- Possess strong mental working capacity, cognitive stamina, and motivation and realize that the ascent to leadership is gradual and must be earned.

In Levine's words, "Such prolonged toil calls for the delay of gratification and the realization that your boss (unlike your mom) doesn't much care if you're having fun. Nor is she or he lying awake at night worrying about your self-esteem" (2007, p. 20).

Interaction

Students with strong interaction skills possess social cognition and can do the following:

- Balance the desire for peer acceptance with the need to develop as a unique individual with distinctive interests, goals, and aspirations.
- Build and sustain productive, fulfilling relationships.
- Communicate and collaborate effectively.
- Relate to people of all ages.

Inner Direction

Students with a strong sense of inner direction are equipped to explore career pathways because they can do the following:

- Understand their personal strengths, weaknesses, and affinities.
- Recognize personal assets and interests.

Preparing Students for the Future

The gear in Levine's cognitive backpack is consistent with research findings about skills for the future. The Conference Board of Canada (2000), in its *Employability Skills 2000+* document, articulates three specific skill areas that must be developed to successfully enter, stay in, and progress in the world of work:

1. **Fundamental Skills**—Skills needed as a base for further development

   - Communicate.
   - Manage information.

- Use numbers.

- Think and solve problems.

2. **Personal Management Skills**—Personal skills, attitudes, and behaviors that drive one's potential for growth

- Demonstrate positive attitudes and behaviors.

- Be responsible.

- Be adaptable.

- Learn continuously.

- Work safely.

3. **Teamwork Skills**—Skills and attributes needed to contribute productively

- Work with others.

- Participate in projects and tasks.

The Benefits of Strong School-Home-Community Relationships

James Comer (2005) asserted that "student academic performance, behavior and preparation for school and life can be greatly improved when the adult stakeholders work together in a respectful, collaborative way to create a school climate or culture that supports development, good instruction, and academic learning" (p. 39). He stressed the importance of educators consciously nurturing relationships with parents and identified three levels of participation to expect.

Level One: Parents provide general support.

- Attending parent-teacher conferences

- Monitoring homework

- Supporting fundraising activities

- Participating in calendar events such as concerts

Level Two: Parents serve as volunteers in daily school affairs.

- Providing office support

- Going along on field trips

- Working in the library

Level Three: Parents participate in school decision-making by serving on school committees.

Involvement with the school can hold personal benefits for parents as well. Through participation in committee work, parents may discover competencies they were not using and develop skills such as using an agenda, soliciting input from all members, considering the pros and cons of issues, prioritizing, decision-making, and communicating constructively. Parental connection to the school extends the mission of learning by all.

The Other Side of the Report Card

Social, emotional, and character development are the "other side" of the report card. While schools have a central role in developing the nonacademic side of the student, the most profound influence comes from their families. Sometimes that influence is positive, and sometimes it is not. When it is positive, parents and teachers can work as partners to help students develop in a socially positive way. When it is less than positive, the role of the school becomes even more critical. In such cases, teachers and other members of the community must become the student's primary role models and supporters. Specialized character education and social awareness programs are useful for all children and provide a forum for discussion about such things as bullying, risky behaviors, and social responsibility. Mentorship with positive role models and hands-on experience with providing service to the community are also effective for developing socioemotional competence and character.

Many schools provide parents with training on parenting topics such as helping students with homework, supporting literacy and numeracy at home, talking to teenagers, watching for and responding to signs of drug involvement and other risky behaviors, and bullying. It is important that schools reach out to parents to learn how they can best support and promote parental involvement—for the benefit of students.

The Importance of Leadership

As you have read in previous chapters, shared vision is a necessary, but insufficient prerequisite for leadership. To be effective, leadership must be distributed throughout the school community. It must be based on trust and a belief that no one has all of the knowledge, skill, or energy to lead single-handedly. Adults working together toward a shared vision can pool their skills as well as their unique strengths and personalities to make a difference for all students within their care.

Reeves (2006) validated the importance of distributed leadership and extended it by making the point that all adults within a school community, regardless of title or position, have a role to play in creating and sustaining an environment that is conducive to learning by all. He asserted that bus drivers and cafeteria workers ought to be involved in professional development sessions about discipline and student motivation because for many students, the school day starts on the bus or when having breakfast, not in the classroom. Sessions about literacy should include custodians and administrative assistants so that they can join the rest of the staff in supporting student literacy growth and modeling the joy of reading. In Reeves' view, "every class is an opportunity for students to engage in creativity, literacy, project organization, personal responsibility, teamwork and a host of other skills that will contribute to their success. . . . and there is no such thing as a 'nonacademic' class, assembly or experience" (2006, p. 30). When leadership is distributed, every certified and noncertified staff member supports a common focus on improving teaching and learning. Parents and members of the broader community are important supporters, too.

What the Lesson Teaches Us

- Educators are profoundly influential in preparing children and youth for adulthood.

- Collaborative relationships with parents and the broader community can support the work that educators do to prepare students for adulthood.

- To address the whole child, learning must go beyond academics.

- The world into which students will graduate is diverse and constantly changing.

- Students must prepare to become citizens of the world.

- Parents and the community can most effectively address student needs by working in partnership.

- School staff must work deliberately to forge partnerships with parents and the community.

- School leaders can help teachers develop positive, constructive relationships with parents.

- Members of the community may be directly involved with students at the school level or involved through providing service and financial support.

- To be adequately prepared as start-up adults, students must have a cognitive "backpack" loaded with the mental skills of interpretation, instrumentation, interaction, and inner direction.

- The Conference Board of Canada identifies fundamental skills, personal management skills, and teamwork skills as requisites for the future.

- The depth of parent participation in school activities will vary according to their interest, skill, and availability.

- Parents have much to offer and gain from involvement with the school.

- Social, emotional, and character development represent the "other side" of the report card.

- While families have a critical impact on the nonacademic side of student development, educators also have a central role to play.

- Schools can support families through providing programs on parenting topics.

- Adults working together to achieve a shared vision of the preparation students must have for the future can have a powerful impact on their learning and development.

Lessons Lived: Stories From the Real World

Although it is very important, academic achievement is only one aspect of student growth. The schools written about in this section have effectively worked in partnership with parents and the community at large to ensure that their students have opportunities that will facilitate every aspect of their development as individuals. They are representative of early, middle, and senior years' educational settings.

G. L. Roberts Collegiate and Vocational Institute

G. L. Roberts Collegiate and Vocational Institute serves 785 students from grades 9–12 in Oshawa, Ontario. Of the students, 29% are identified as having special needs, 37% are enrolled in academic/university destination courses, 49% are in applied/college destination courses, and 12% take essential/workplace destination courses. The staff of G. L. Roberts totals 74, including 58 teachers and 16 educational assistants. Principal Ian Skinner and Vice Principal Vicky Pidgeon believe, "It is people and then programs that make a great school." Under the effective schools umbrella, they work with the staff to do whatever it takes to provide students with the experiences, opportunities, and instruction they need to achieve personal, social, and academic success.

The Socio-Economic Risk Index is a composite index of measures of socioeconomic status that mark living and/or working conditions that place people at risk. At G.L. Roberts, the vast majority of the school's student population is split between high risk and somewhat high risk, with small pockets of moderate and low risk. Many of the students have limited background experience, low self-esteem, and difficult life issues. These students do not perceive that postsecondary training will be an option for them. The staff is committed to finding ways to involve students in activities and learning experiences that will not only enhance student skill levels, but will also boost their sense of personal efficacy and hope for the future. Belonging, recognition, encouragement, and support are key ingredients of the G. L. Roberts school culture. Ian states, "Our staff is dedicated to our students. They strive to continuously improve instruction, programs, and support, and make decisions focused on achieving success for all students." They are guided by a shared vision of "learning for all . . . whatever it takes."

Whatever It Takes: Involving All Partners to Make It Work

There is no doubt that learning for all students is a priority at G. L. Roberts. The staff has found many ways to develop the employability skills as identified by the Conference Board of Canada. To include all of them here would not be practical, but a few stand out as particularly powerful.

Saturn Camp. The Saturn Camp tradition at G. L. Roberts exemplifies a culture characterized by positive leadership, interdependence, and collaboration between staff, students, administration, and the community. Each year, a 3-day residential camp experience takes grade 9 students to a rural camp setting where they are supervised by senior student leaders (counselors) working in partnership with key teachers and camp staff. Camp activities focus on skill-building in the areas of interpersonal relationships, teamwork, and leadership. Students return from camp having made new friends and acquired new skills. Their shared experience results in a sense of belonging to the school and a camaraderie that lasts long after camp is over. A tangible example of the spirit that builds at camp is the "Cha Cha Slide." Prior to each meal at camp, students do the camp dance, the Cha Cha Slide. Even years after they have attended the camp, students instantly break into the dance when they hear the music at school activities. Saturn Camp is always a topic central to speeches at prom and graduation ceremonies.

Saturn Camp is a powerful experience for students and has an extremely positive effect on the overall climate of the school. Many students who attend the camp return with the goal of serving as Saturn Camp counselors in their senior years. Camp alumni are a significant portion of students taking leadership courses, working as peer mentors, and assuming leadership roles in school clubs and other activities. In fact, data show that attendance at the camp assists with reducing dropout rates (see Table 8-1).

Table 8-1: Retention Rates at G. L. Roberts

	Saturn Camp Attendees	Non-Attendees
2001	78.0%	N/A
2002	80.8%	57.5%
2003	90.5%	74.2%
2004	92.8%	72.5%

Community support is the key to making the camp experience possible. Generous sponsorship from Motorcity Saturn, a local car dealership, covers the majority of related costs. To raise additional funds, staff and students organize an annual Roberts Roast, which is a roast beef dinner (prepared and served by students with food donated by the community and staff-connected businesses) and silent auction (prizes supplied through donations received from staff and community sponsors due to staff and student efforts). Entertainment for the event is donated by former graduates. Staff and students identify Saturn Camp as a critical component of their school culture and one that must be continued into the future.

Horticultural Program. Ian states that the Horticultural Program "is representative of our move to practical, career-based programming and the positive impact of this on the students and school." This program provides an opportunity for all students, regardless of whether they plan to complete postsecondary education. It includes a range of courses pertaining to horticulture that are based on student interest. Courses are designed to facilitate either workplace or college entry. In response to the success of the Horticultural Program, the Ontario Youth Apprenticeship Program Horticulture is now offered at G. L. Roberts in partnership with Humber College and Landscape

Ontario. Effective in 2007–08, students could graduate with a major in horticulture as a result of the school receiving industry certification and providing cooperative education experiences in local horticulture settings.

The Horticultural Program has an 85% completion rate and has had many positive side benefits for students. For example, the number of students in the school's Horticultural Club has doubled. Students have designed, created, and maintained gardens around the school. Members of the community recently nominated G. L. Roberts for the Communities in Bloom Award. In addition, the Oshawa City Council nominated the school for the Jessica Markland Award for Environmental Partnership from the Durham Environmental Advisory Committee in 2006, and the school won. The Horticultural Program and activities associated with it seem to have taken on a life of their own. The success of the school gardens has resulted in community partnerships to design other gardens, such as a butterfly garden in Oshawa. The staff and students involved are presently working with the City of Oshawa and other community groups on the revitalization and redevelopment of a park and marsh area adjacent to the school as well as the landscaping for the new South Oshawa Community Centre, which is attached to and operates in partnership with the school and the Durham District School Board.

Data collected from students confirmed the effectiveness of the Horticultural Program:

- 75% stated they learned best through hands-on activities.

- 77.8% claimed that their part in developing the G. L. Roberts gardens made them feel more proud of their school.

- 88.9% felt that the horticulture course made them feel better about their skills.

- 75% stated that the course made them feel better about coming to school.

- 96.3% stated they would like to see more practical courses like this at the school.

- 89.3% claimed they now know more about job opportunities available in horticulture and landscaping.

- 39.3% said that their attendance improved this semester compared to last semester.

Roberts Gardens. In 2005–06, the Horticultural Program paired with the manufacturing technology, design technology, and graphic design programs to establish a model business they called "Roberts Gardens." To get started, a group including teachers, the special education and technology heads, and administrators formed a committee, established an account for the business, created a business plan, and implemented the business plan. The committee set regular dates to monitor and review progress, to establish products to be marketed, and to determine prices relative to production costs. A product promotion campaign including signs, posters, and a display was developed to launch Roberts Gardens at a parent night.

A number of horticultural products have been successfully designed, manufactured, and marketed by the students and staff of Roberts Gardens. These products have proven to be popular and are now marketed by student volunteers at community events, such as Earth Day and the South Oshawa Pride Day, in partnership with the City of Oshawa and other community agencies. Funds raised have been used to sustain the project and support practical programs. The business involves students in the design, manufacturing, and marketing of a line of outdoor garden ornaments as well as the creation and maintenance of perennial gardens that will eventually provide plants for sale. Through involvement in Roberts Gardens, students learn about entrepreneurship, design, manufacturing, and marketing. This has been a highly successful program and business. Through it, students have learned about entrepreneurship and fiscal responsibility—it has provided real-world experience for them.

Literacy Initiatives. "Literacy is good!" is the motto for the Literacy Committee. Comprised of cross-departmental staff, the Literacy Committee is a large professional learning community that oversees all literacy initiatives in the school and has divided into subcommittees or teams in order to support a variety of needed interventions.

Subcommittees of the Literacy Committee

- Community Outreach
- Student Literacy
- Literacy Test Simulation
- Test Day Breakfast
- Literacy Practice Packages
- Family of Schools Involvement

- Parent Contact and Information
- Schoolwide Silent Reading Program
- Literacy Test Day Simulation
- Literacy Test Remediation and Preparation
- Spring Training (literacy carnival)

The Literacy Committee takes the initiative for numerous activities that promote literacy in the school, including organizing relevant professional development, running a "You've been booked" campaign during which students caught reading are entered in a drawing for prizes, and promoting regular silent reading breaks in the school. Perhaps their most intensive work lies in preparing students for the Ontario Secondary School Literacy Test (OSSLT), which is administered to grade 10 students. Although the school operates on a semester system, test preparation activities occur throughout the year. The following list provides an overview of their activities:

- The committee uses a previous OSSLT test as a practice test. Eligible students from grade 10 or any senior student who still needs a successful test result to graduate write the practice exam in November. A Student Literacy Committee assists the teachers involved with organization and setup of this and other literacy activities.

- The Test Day Simulation Committee meets in December to mark the tests using the rubrics provided.

- Practice test results are tabulated, and a student list is created that guides instruction. Trends are shared with the committee to guide and adapt OSSLT preparation activities.

- In January, students receive individual reports with marks, comments, and guidance about where to focus their efforts prior to the actual OSSLT, which is written in March.

- The entire Literacy Committee meets to review work and plan.

- The preparation subcommittee meets to prepare two half-day sessions, one focused on reading skills and one on writing skills. These sessions are held in February for students who had difficulty on the pretest and are designed to address the gaps revealed on the practice test. Teacher volunteers lead and supervise the sessions, with support from educational assistants.

- The parent contact subcommittee makes calls to parents to inform them of the March test and to enlist their support in encouraging their children to do their best.

- Literacy Spring Training is held in March for all students who will be writing the test. The spring training subcommittee organizes a half-day interactive session that covers all sections of the test to develop reading, writing, and "test-attack" strategies. Twelve teacher-coaches from across departments volunteer to provide training for a total of 250 students. In one activity, for example, coaches cut the sentences from an essay expressing opinion into strips. Students work in groups to decide on and present the correct order for the sentences. All students win prizes. Balloons and music make the atmosphere festive.

- On the day of the test, the school provides breakfast for all students. Teachers join them in the cafeteria to provide encouragement and cheer them as they exit to go to test rooms. While students are writing the test, teachers pass out juice, water, and cookies. Students with an IEP are given extended time to write the test, and they are given cheese, crackers, and fruit to fuel their efforts.

- When the test results arrive in June, committee members compare them to the fall simulated test results to gauge the effectiveness of the preparation activities and to results from previous years to collect information for future planning. Continuous improvement is the goal.

Looking Back With Satisfaction

The staff of G. L. Roberts is dedicated to finding ways to help all students succeed socially, emotionally, and intellectually and to developing leadership skills in students and staff. Inclusivity is highly valued. Students have many opportunities and are strongly encouraged to become involved in the life of the school. The number of practical, career-based programs is increasing and complements a full range of academic courses. This section provides only a surface look at the kinds of programs, practices, and structures that have been adopted by the staff to promote student success and accomplish their goal of learning for all . . . whatever it takes. Ian Skinner moved into a central office position with the Durham District School Board in the spring of 2008, ready to cooperate with other schools in the district to make it work for kids and confident that the good work will continue at G. L. Roberts.

Rockcliffe Middle School

Kevin Battaglia became the principal of Rockcliffe Middle School in 2002. Rockcliffe is located in Toronto, Ontario, and has a highly diverse population of 407 students in grades 6–8, representing more than 40 different nationalities. Approximately 8% of the students have lived in Canada for fewer than 5 years, and 51% of the students are English-language learners. The staff consists of 23 teachers and six support staff.

Kevin and the staff of Rockcliffe have developed a clearly stated mission, goal, and motto to guide their work together. They are committed to ensuring that Rockcliffe is a great place to be and an exciting place to learn. Rockcliffe Middle School offers strong academic, arts, and athletic programs. Student progress is closely monitored, and expectations for students are high.

The Rockcliffe mission: To help our students develop personally, intellectually, and socially in order to meet the challenges of an ever-changing world.

The Rockcliffe goal: To authentically engage all students by instilling confidence, broadening horizons, and mentoring students to develop habits which lead to success.

The Rockcliffe motto: Learning for all . . . whatever it takes!

Learning for All . . . Involving Many Partners

The staff employs many, varied strategies and programs to support and encourage their students. They also look beyond the school for support in their work with the result that they have many community partners assisting them to offer vital learning experiences for their students. Several partnership examples are particularly noteworthy within the context of this lesson for school success.

Parents as Partners. At Rockcliffe, parents are considered to be partners in the education of their children. Communication with them is a priority, and a number of effective practices have been established to ensure that their opinions are heard and that they are aware of what is happening in their child's school life. In addition to involvement in parent council meetings and regular parent-teacher conferences, partnership with Rockcliffe parents is nurtured in these ways:

- Parent Speak is a survey and communication tool distributed twice a year to parents to gain insights into their perspectives regarding student achievement, school safety, and communication with the school. As a result of information gathered through Parent Speak, the school has responded by—

◊ Developing comprehensive assessment and homework policies that provide parents with information about the reasons for homework, what constitutes good homework, and how parents can support their children

◊ Developing community and school safety initiatives (such as parking lot safety)

◊ Developing special events to address concerns raised through Parent Speak surveys, such as cyberbullying and how to talk with teens

• Current Standing Reports are mini report cards that are mailed home halfway through each term. This practice began when staff observed a noticeable improvement in student achievement immediately following report-card time. They concluded that when parents had a written report from the school, they were better able to focus supervision and mentorship for school success. The Current Standing Report practice has been in place at Rockcliffe since 2003. During that time, parents have expressed no concerns about being surprised when the formal report card arrives home. In Kevin's words, "The staff has embraced the idea that if we are to have lasting success with our students, parents must be authentic partners in our efforts. The staff understands that for many parents whose own education was not highly successful, we need to make the first move, second move, and third move to ensure that they get on board with doing all we can both at home and at school to foster student success."

• Red/Yellow List is a weekly monitoring and communication tool for all students that was used for the second and third years of Kevin's time as principal at Rockcliffe. Every Friday, staff members identified any students who had failed to meet their academic or behavioral expectations. Those students were temporarily withdrawn from cocurricular activities until they could demonstrate that they were able and willing to live up to the expectations that had been set for them. Written documentation was mailed to parents identifying the problem areas and inviting communication with the school. The Red/Yellow List strategy was used to change the culture of the building from one of entitlement to one of working to achieve goals. As the end of the third year approached, the staff realized that they had made such gains toward their goals that they felt they no longer needed this schoolwide system in place to motivate students to make positive choices. In Kevin's words, "Any extrinsic reward system has a limited shelf life. The Red/Yellow List strategy helped to address specific concerns. Its purpose was to make itself obsolete—and it did."

- The Homework Hotline provides an opportunity for parents to contact a Rockcliffe teacher on a special phone to learn what homework has been assigned. Students can use the hotline to seek assistance with homework.

Power Snack and Start Time. The staff identified that many students were coming to school without breakfast, and then trying to do the academic equivalent of taking a 6-hour drive with very little gas in the tank. Many were arriving late and frazzled due to a hectic morning at home and poor time management. The school took two steps to address the identified problems:

1. Daily, at 10:20 a.m., all students are offered a healthy snack (such as fruit, yogurt, or a bagel). Within 2 weeks of implementing this program, teachers reported a significant increase in time on task in late-morning periods, a noticeable decrease in student irritability, and a noticeable improvement in late-morning academic assessment results. Teachers are very pleased with the effect of the power snack, and parents are overwhelmingly supportive as well, commenting that they struggle to get their kids to eat breakfast. Parents also commented that they had difficulty getting their children to eat fruits and vegetables at home and were relieved to know that they were getting them at school.

2. Start time has been pushed back by 10 minutes each day except for Monday, when it is pushed back by 30 minutes. Many students were chronically late because they are responsible for walking younger siblings to school and were reluctant to leave them before adult supervision was in place. The 30-minute late start on Monday was implemented in recognition that Monday mornings are often challenging for families as they struggle to get the weekly routine back in place. The later start times compensate for these issues and make it possible for students to arrive at school on time.

Boys to Men. When Kevin came to Rockcliffe, he obtained district support to initiate a Boys to Men (B2M) mentorship program as a fundamental component of his entry plan. He had previous experience with the program in two other schools and believed passionately in its potential to "override aspects of the cultural environment that exist outside of the school" through providing grade 8 boys with supportive mentorship, learning experiences, and opportunities to be engaged in prosocial activities. At first, the program had a cocurricular focus in areas such as boys' book clubs, boys' nights, small group talks, special trips, retreats, events, and guest speakers. From the group that participated in these activities, the staff identified specific students and began to focus small-group activities on such things as anger management, building healthy relationships, and organizational skills. By Kevin's third year at Rockcliffe, he and the staff recognized that they needed to do more than offer cocurricular activities to the boys. The result was the creation of a grade 8 B2M class, an all-boys class that is self-contained during the school day.

The rationale behind B2M is that boys are more likely than girls to become high risk, especially as they approach adolescence. Kevin quotes the work of author and therapist Michael Gurian, who says that more boys than girls report being less interested in school. Boys constitute over 90% of suspensions, are more likely to be described as disruptive, aggressive, or violent, and are underrepresented in school student leadership roles. Boys' reading and writing skills lag behind those of girls; they are more likely to repeat a grade and drop out before graduation. They are three times more likely than girls to be in special education programs and four times more likely to be diagnosed with ADHD (attention deficit hyperactivity disorder). Crime and life-skills issues are also major concerns for boys. The majority of child abuse victims are boys, and they are more likely to become addicted to drugs and alcohol. The vast majority of crimes are committed by boys, and 90% of those in jail are male. Ninety percent of males who impregnate a teenage girl abandon her and the child. Adolescent males are four times more likely to commit suicide than girls (Gurian, 2001). The B2M program is staffed by male Rockcliffe staff members who see themselves as mentors. These teachers believe that "you cannot teach them until you reach them." They earn respect by modeling integrity and character, offering every student personal advice and learning support. The B2M curriculum focuses on student success and pathways to the future. Following are some of the activities and teaching components of the program:

- Boys participate in a 3-day retreat at the beginning of the year to build teamwork skills through kayaking, rock climbing, team challenges, and problem-solving initiatives.

- B2M provides exposure to the Roots of Empathy program, which teaches about infant care and development. The majority of boys in B2M live in fatherless homes. Roots of Empathy challenges them to define their image of fatherhood and envision what it could mean to them as a man. The boys are helped to understand that any male can be a father, but that only a "real man" can be a dad.

- Through a mentorship arrangement with a nearby elementary school, the boys support students identified as at risk in grades 1 and 2.

- Literacy initiatives include subscriptions to magazines of high interest to the boys, as well as novel studies that focus on life lessons and character development.

- Boys participate in daily structured physical education (P.E.) classes. (All schools are required to provide 20 minutes of physical activity daily—however, this is not necessarily structured P.E. time.)

- Politics 101 is designed to teach the boys about the democratic process through discussion and field experience.

- Stock Market Math enriches the regular math curriculum through the study of money management and the stock market.

- In Chef in the Classroom, Junior Charles, a professional chef who is also a certified Toastmaster, works with the boys to prepare a formal banquet at which they wear shirts and ties to present the speeches he coaches them to deliver.

- Juan Alvarez, a former El Salvadorian refugee who spent most of his alienated youth creating graffiti art around the city, has developed his urban art into a successful computer graphics business and serves as a successful role model to the boys.

- Paul Green developed a program, Urban Media Analysis, aimed at increasing the boys' abilities to be critical consumers. The program revolves around analyzing lyrics of rap songs and images of manhood found in advertising, movies, and videos.

- Fashion designer Curtis James exposed the boys to his creative process and shared the successes and challenges of entrepreneurship in fashion design.

Outcomes of the B2M Program Participants
• 93% of students had reduced tardiness and/or absences.
• 83% met all curricular requirements for grade 8.
• 100% had fewer office referrals and suspensions.
Compared with grade 8 boys in other classes, those in B2M achieved significantly better results in all areas: achievement, attitudes, attendance, and behaviors.

The B2M program is clearly a success. It demonstrates that a single-sex grouping for boys at risk is a powerful way to re-engage them. Working with teachers who define themselves as mentors, learning activities that are tailored to meet their needs, and being exposed to positive role models and pathways for success helps the boys to prepare for a positive future.

Balancing Academics and Sports in Education. Balancing Academics and Sports in Education (BASE) is a community outreach program that provides students with an opportunity to be positively engaged between 3:30 and 7:00 p.m. Students play cooperative games, do homework with support, have dinner, and participate in sports, arts, or technology-related activities. The BASE program is staffed by a child and youth worker along with volunteer high school students. It is housed at Rockcliffe and made possible through sponsorship by an anonymous community donor.

Looking Back With Satisfaction

In the time that Kevin has been at Rockcliffe Middle School, he has helped implement a wide array of practices and structures that are tangible evidence of commitment to their stated mission, goal, and motto. Kevin says:

> I try to lead from a combination of my head and my heart. I survey, I ask, I track lates, suspensions, and office referrals, and have endless ways of determining academic success, including the Canadian Achievement Test and the Rockcliffe Test of Basic Writing Skills. I talk to parents, teachers, students, and other stakeholders, asking, "What do you think about this idea? How has this program helped you? What can we do better together?"

Kevin is proud of the work that is being done on behalf of Rockcliffe students. He says that he leads "a group of exceptional teachers who are passionately committed to improving the lives of the young people they teach."

Kevin was promoted in the fall of 2007 to a central administrator position within the Safe and Caring Schools Department of the Toronto District School Board. In his new position, he is working to provide the same type of programming and opportunities to district students who have been suspended or expelled.

Somerset and District Elementary School

Somerset and District Elementary School situated in Berwick, Nova Scotia, serves 11 diverse rural communities and has a population of 210 K–6 students. According to the school, close to 25% of the students at Somerset come from single-parent families. The transience rate is high, and many families live at or below the poverty line. The staff of Somerset consists of nine classroom teachers as well as six part-time specialist teachers in music, physical education, reading recovery, resource, French, and guidance. Six educational assistants work in a variety of ways with identified students. Heather Morse is the principal.

The staff of Somerset is guided by a clearly articulated belief: "We believe a safe, caring and secure environment gives all an opportunity to develop to their full potential academically, socially and emotionally."

Learning for All . . . Many Partners Working Together

In keeping with their belief statement, the Somerset staff has taken many steps to ensure that the scope of teaching at their school extends beyond an academic focus to foster skills that will help students grow and become successful adults. At the classroom level, the focus is on academic achievement, particularly in literacy and numeracy; however, Somerset places an equally strong emphasis on providing experiences beyond the classroom to develop confidence, resilience, and a sense of personal efficacy.

The Systems Approach to a Violence-Free Environment (SAVE) has been operating successfully at Somerset since 1995–96. The family, school, and community work together to ensure that the school provides a supportive and nurturing learning environment where both adults and children feel safe and respected. A SAVE Advisory Committee meets once a year to hear what the school has been doing, give input, and direct future initiatives. A school-based SAVE committee meets monthly to develop and support in-school activities.

SAVE Advisory Committee Members

- Students (present and former)
- Home and school representatives
- Parents
- Bus drivers
- Family and Children Services representative(s)
- Child and Adolescent Services representative(s)
- Member(s) of the Royal Canadian Mounted Police
- Local church pastors
- Board of Trade representative
- Department of Health representative
- School board representatives
- Social Action Committee representatives from local churches
- Program consultant from the school district
- School principal
- Teacher representatives

Since SAVE has been in operation, many initiatives have been developed and implemented—too many to detail here. The following appear to have had an ongoing, positive impact.

Student Leadership. Peer mediators help those experiencing conflict to solve their problems. Student leaders in grades 4–6 are selected by their peers to become mediators based on their abilities to listen, treat others respectfully, and maintain confidentiality. They are trained to help people arrive at a win-win solution to their problems.

Students in grades 5 and 6 work with teachers to help keep the playground safe and fun. Each week, Heather, the principal, works with students to develop a schedule of daily activities for students. Examples of such activities include road hockey, knee hockey, fun with computers, toy club, soccer, and baseball.

Funds from the Department of Health provided a facilitator who trained 12 students in the Bully Busters program: how to recognize and respond to bullying. As part of this funded initiative, teachers also led classroom-based lessons using program materials.

Health Promoting School Initiative. The staff of Somerset was instrumental in the development of what is known as the Health Promoting School Initiative, which currently exists in all 43 schools in the Annapolis Valley. Somerset has also provided leadership for the Active and Healthy Living program sponsored by the Annapolis Valley Regional School Board.

The Somerset Breakfast Club provides breakfast daily at 8:00 a.m. for children who arrive at school without having eaten and for those who leave from home very early in order to ride the bus to school. A healthy snack canteen provides additional nutritional support by selling snacks at cost during recess and noon every day of the week. Nova Scotia Health Promotion and Protection, in cooperation with Somerset Home and School, helps to fund a food services coordinator to oversee all aspects of the food program. Other sponsors for the food program are the Canadian Living Foundation (Breakfast for Learning), Feed My Lambs Social Action Group, donations from the District Dress Down Committee, the Children's Emergency Foundation, and the Home and School Association.

Exploratories. One afternoon a week, all grade 5 and 6 students participate in activities that allow them to explore new activities and pastimes. Groups of 6–20 students explore activities that operate for a period of 6 to 8 weeks. Transportation, supplies, honoraria, and facility rentals are made possible through the support of the Home and School Association.

One of the most celebrated outcomes of SAVE is the ownership students take of their school. When a need for new playground equipment was identified, students approached the Home and School Association for support. They surveyed all classes for suggestions about desired equipment, and they encouraged their parents to become involved in the project. When funding came available for the new equipment, the grade 3 class wrote to the Home and School Association offering to help with the planning for its installation. Students also worked with parents to design a sign for their school. Through this kind of involvement with adults, students have become comfortable at meetings, listening and discussing the issues at hand with intelligence and respect.

Examples of Exploratories

- Adopting a grandparent at a senior's complex
- Adopting a preschooler at a local daycare center
- Adopting a buddy at the Kings County Rehabilitation Centre
- Curling classes
- Bully Busters (learning to teach others about dealing with bullying)
- Cooking classes
- Kinder-skills classes (learning to lead young children in physical activities)
- Red Cross babysitting course
- Exploring 4-H
- Exploring art
- Exploring dance
- Active living

Building a Stronger and Safer Community

Beginning in 2003, Somerset piloted a 2-year project with Justice Canada in conjunction with the Durham District School Board. "Together We Light the Way: Building Stronger and Safer Communities" complemented and enhanced the work being done through the SAVE program. The goals of the program were to build resilience and responsibility in children and to increase the protective factors that enhance the likelihood of student success by involving the entire community in working with them. Four pillars—academics, respect, teamwork, and leadership—form the foundation for the program.

At Somerset, the funding that came with the pilot project paid for Canadian Achievement Testing (CAT), a beneficial and welcomed addition to the assessment program currently in place at the school. Funding also supported staff trainers, teaching materials, and researchers to conduct surveys and assist with evaluating the project.

The success of the Together We Light the Way: Building Stronger and Safer Communities pilot project was evidenced by these outcomes:

- Reading achievement scores increased at all grade levels. Math achievement increased at some, but not all, grade levels.

Protective Factors Enhance the Likelihood of Student Success

- School success

- Increased academic achievement

- Sense of self-worth

- Safe, secure, and nurturing environments

- Healthful lifestyle

- Positive family and school relationships

- Respectful and caring relationships

- Connection to caring adults

- Reported incidences of inappropriate language, physical assaults, and vandalism decreased significantly.

- Reported bullying of a socioemotional nature decreased significantly as children became more confident about coming forward for help.

- Students reported in student surveys that they felt happier and more successful at school. They said they felt cared for and supported in their studies.

- Parent and guardian survey results indicated increased satisfaction with—

  ◊ Their children's reading, writing, and computer skills

  ◊ Teacher support of their children's learning

  ◊ Fair treatment of students and consistent expectations for student behavior

  ◊ The school's extracurricular offerings

  ◊ Opportunities for parents to be involved in decision-making

  ◊ The welcoming climate in the school

- Staff survey feedback indicated that they view parents as their partners.

- Teachers were 100% consistently positive about school safety on the staff survey. They observed positive shifts in student self-worth, efforts to decrease bullying, and respectful interactions among people.

- Formal community partnerships increased significantly, from 26 to 55. Involvement of individual volunteers also increased.

Although the pilot project has ended, the staff, students, and community of Somerset remain focused on fostering the safer and stronger community they have built. In the words of one of the students, "Basically, it's about respect. To me, it's being respectful and helping other people to be respectful. It helps us set goals to grow more academically and socially."

Looking Back With Satisfaction

A significant strength at Somerset and District Elementary School is the supportive and collaborative relationships that have been developed with the community. Heather Morse is passionate about providing the best possible education for all children, particularly those at risk. In her words, "All partners must come together and make a collective effort to take what we think we know about child poverty, consider it critically, and envision how it might be otherwise." With significant support from parents and the community, Heather and the staff are making a difference for the children in their care.

Summary

To help students develop the skills they will need to be successful adults, a focus on academic skills is important but insufficient. Student learning must extend beyond academics to include the competencies necessary for personal management and teamwork in a rapidly changing world. When strong collaborative relationships are built among all of the adults in the school and extended to parents and the broader community, the responsibility for meeting the various needs of all students is shared. Instructional leadership that is distributed is necessary to provide the impetus for developing important school-home-community relationships.

The work of individual schools is greatly enhanced when senior administrators and elected officials of the school district share the same values and work in concert with one another. Chapter 9 is about instructional leadership, this time at the senior administrative level.

Creating Communities of Hope

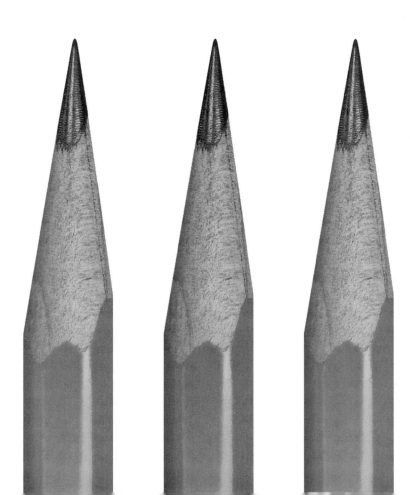

Expect Rocks and Hard Places . . .
They Are Inevitable

In Section 2, we wrote about Harbors of Hope that reside in many different districts in cities, towns, and rural areas in all parts of Canada. Their stories highlight the lessons for school success we have identified, and they demonstrate their application in the pursuit of the mission of learning for all. Change challenges the old and understood ways of operating, so it was no surprise to hear from the schools that their journey was not without trials and tribulations. The road taken when planning for school improvement is seldom smooth and uneventful because it forces people outside of their comfort zones. They must leave behind the tried, true, and comfortable to engage in new learning and new practices that may, at least initially, challenge their feelings of competence. The transition from old to new can be very uncomfortable, and the temptation to revert to old ways is strong. It is a process that is rife with highs and lows. Rocks and hard places are inevitable.

Through our work with the schools featured in Section 2, it became obvious that leadership at the district level is an important determinant of each school's ability to address challenges in order to get better—not just get by. Those districts with a comprehensive, coherent plan to support improved teaching and learning in *all* schools are most able to support school improvement efforts effectively. These districts are aligned for success. As a result, rocks and hard places at the school level are not nearly as numerous or onerous.

In an aligned district, the elected officials, senior administration, school administrators, and school staff all agree on the mission, core beliefs, and core values that underpin the system. Superintendents, directors, and other centrally appointed staff are the keys to creating this alignment; they are in positions to listen to and understand the needs of the schools, community, and province. Based on what they ascertain, they can create policies, procedures, and strategies that will have a positive impact on the district as a whole.

The perspective and management style of senior administrators and directors have a significant impact on the climate of the district as a whole. When central office leaders focus on command, control, and conform strategies, the outcome is compliance and loss of enthusiasm. On the other hand, when central office leaders see themselves as servants to the needs that exist in the district, they will focus on making a difference for students, teachers, and the community they serve. In districts that are aligned for success, collaboration, coordination, and communication are the norm. The outcome is change, growth, and the celebration of success for all students. Staff members are professionally enthused. The community trusts the system. In these districts, instructional leadership at the senior administration level is a priority—and that leadership is shared throughout the district.

The Link to Effective Schools Research

In *Assembly Required* (Lezotte & McKee, 2002), the authors identified an understanding of system thinking as a critical component of sustainable school reform. They explained that "system thinking is a network of interdependent components that work together to accomplish the aim of the system" (p. 8). They went on to say that the current system is difficult to change. In most school districts, there are five barriers (pp. 26–28) that must be confronted before getting better can become a certainty:

1. **Public education is a classic top-down bureaucracy.** It is a command-and-control system in which the authority rests at the top and the accountability at the bottom.

2. **Public education is a deeply layered system.** Students are nested in classrooms; classrooms are nested in schools; schools are nested in districts; and districts nested in provinces and states. This nesting is a major obstacle to the two-way flow of information between those with authority and those who are accountable.

3. **Public education has an enormous amount of inertia.** The current system is usually predictable, characterized by apathy and lack of interest in change.

4. **Public education, like other systems, strives to maintain balance in the status quo.** The current system is not only resistant to change, but actively strives to ensure that things stay the same as they have always been. By seeing fundamental change as a

disruption or threat instead of an opportunity to improve, public education is at risk of destroying itself.

5. **The system of public education, like other systems, is held in place by anchors.** The anchors in the public education system are the local school board and the communities it represents, as well as the school administrators, the teachers, and the associations and unions that represent them. To create sustainable change in the system in place, the permission and support of the stakeholder groups are essential.

> In schools that are Harbors of Hope, learning by all is a reality. In these schools, the correlates work in concert and are interdependent. All seven are consistently present and powerfully demonstrated.

Lezotte and McKee (2002) asserted that "creating the organizational culture that supports continuous school improvement will be the key to the long-term sustainable success of public education" (p. 199). Senior administrators have a critical role to play in the creation of that culture. It behooves them to take an active role as instructional leaders to make certain that the correlates are as influential at the system level as they are at the individual school level. Administrators must ensure that everyone understands the mission and core values of the district. They must also accept responsibility for mining the data on school and student success and for developing a plan to ensure that school administrators and teachers have the knowledge and skills necessary to deliver on the mission. Strong instructional leadership is as imperative at the district level as it is at the school level.

Effective schools research tells us that an effective model of sustainable school improvement is:

- Results-oriented

- Focused on both quality and equity

- Data-driven

- Research-based

- Collaborative

- Ongoing and self-renewing

What We Have Learned About the Lesson

Most of us have at one time or another experienced the pain of mis-alignment. Perhaps the tires on a car wore out too quickly because the wheels were not aligned, or maybe a back gave out and made even the smallest aspects of daily living a chore. When organizations are misaligned, every member pays a price in frustration as well as loss of motivation and personal satisfaction. The importance of alignment cannot be overstated.

Over the years, many researchers in education and business have explored the role of senior administrators in the creation of outstanding organizations. W. Edwards Deming, the father of total quality management and continuous improvement, is renowned for his work in this area. In his book *The New Economics for Industry, Government, and Education,* he pointed out the importance of system thinking in improving quality and results:

> The *Appreciation of a system* involves understanding how interactions (i.e. feedback) between the elements of a system can result in internal restrictions that force the system to behave as a single organism that automatically seeks a steady state. It is this steady state that determines the output of the system rather than the individual elements. Thus it is the structure of the organization rather than the employees, alone, which holds the key to improving the quality of output. (Deming, 2000, p. 17)

Peter Senge (1990) introduced the concept of a *learning organization,* an organization that will continue to thrive during times of change and challenge. He outlined the five disciplines or lessons that need to be learned by organizations that want to get better, not just get by. The fifth discipline, systems thinking, integrates the other four for the benefit of the organization.

Five Disciplines
1. Personal mastery
2. Mental models
3. Shared vision
4. Team learning
5. Systems thinking
(Senge, 1990)

Systems thinking is based on the belief that the only way to fully understand why a problem or issue occurs and persists is to understand it in relation to the whole. In this framework, we understand a system by examining the linkages and interactions between all of its elements.

Stephen Covey (1990) asserted that "all organizations are perfectly aligned to get the results they are achieving" (p. 67). He identified four roles that leaders must fill to develop an organization that will thrive:

1. Pathfinding—Determining an organization's purpose, vision, and values

2. Aligning—Ensuring that the structures and processes are in place to allow for success

3. Empowering—Encouraging and providing opportunities for people to take action and make a difference

4. Modeling—Behaving in principle-centered ways so that the other three roles can be realized

When a school system makes it a priority to ensure success for all students, it is imperative that the district leaders look at the structures and processes in place to determine if they support reaching the mission of learning by all. If the mission cannot be achieved, the system is not aligned.

A Framework for Alignment

Childress, Elmore, and Grossman (2006) acknowledged that the most important work that occurs in a school district is the daily classroom interaction between teachers and students. District leaders are uniquely positioned to create conditions that enable teachers and students to consistently perform at high levels by creating a coherent organization characterized by the following conditions:

- A focus on student achievement—This is supported by a solid plan for learning emphasizing teacher professional development and curriculum implementation that optimizes best practices.

- A performance culture—A performance culture is collaborative, based on high expectations and accountability.

- Systems and structures—In a coherent system, things such as reporting relationships, roles and responsibilities, resource allocation, training programs, and mechanisms for ensuring accountability are aligned to be consistent with the mission of learning by all.

- Resources—Staff, money, technology, resources, and data are carefully managed to ensure that they support teaching and learning as well as overall system coherence.

- Stakeholders—Senior administrators think politically in order to make the changes required for alignment, because stakeholders rarely agree on what success looks like. The stakeholder group in education includes teachers' unions, parents, school boards, community and advocacy groups, politicians, and policymakers.

- Environment—Senior administrators work with external partners to ensure that the support they offer is used to support learning and the overall plan for system alignment. External partners represent public and private sources such as business groups, foundations, community-based organizations, or universities.

Childress, Elmore, and Grossman (2006) were convinced that "achieving excellence in every corner" of even the largest districts was possible. When district leaders redefine their roles in terms of instructional leadership, it is possible to create a strategy for teaching and learning and support it with coherent, aligned structures and practices.

Fullan, Bertani, and Quinn (2004) identified 10 crucial components for effective leadership for change at the district level that are closely aligned with the framework presented by Childress, Elmore, and Grossman (see feature box, page 185). In their extensive research in Canada, the United States, and England, they have seen the power of the crucial components for change at work at the district level. At the heart of all successful districtwide improvement are a clear mission and values that make commitment to learning by all nonnegotiable.

Finding the balance between centralization and decentralization poses a significant dilemma for school districts; it is "critical not to err on one side or the other" (Fullan, 2005, p. 79). He identifies four areas in which school districts have a vital role to play in promoting and sustaining school improvement efforts:

1. Districts must take measures to develop school capacity to function autonomously before placing them in a position of having to do so.

Ten Components That Make District Improvement Possible

1. A compelling conceptualization

2. Collective moral purpose

3. Structures to support the work that must be done

4. Capacity-building efforts

5. Lateral (cross-school) capacity-building

6. Ongoing learning

7. Productive conflict

8. A demanding culture

9. External partners

10. Focused financial investments

(Fullan, Bertani, & Quinn, 2004)

2. Districts play a significant role in fostering cross-school (lateral) learning, which has powerful benefits for individual teachers, schools, and the entire district. Lateral networking can occur between schools in the district and beyond.

3. Districts have a moral (and increasingly legal) obligation to intervene with schools that chronically underperform.

4. Tri-level alignment is critical to sustained school improvement. Tri-level refers to the school and its community, the district and the trustees, and the provincial or state educational authority. The district is in the middle of the "tri" and as a result has the primary responsibility for alignment. (Fullan, 2005)

Fullan, Cuttress, and Kilcher (2005) note:

We know from past research that neither top-down, prescriptive strategies nor bottom-up, site-based strategies alone work. What is needed is a blend of the two. In tri-level reform, the district as the mid part of the "tri," is in a vital position to reconcile and harness top-down and bottom-up forces needed for large-scale reform. In essence, this is what unlocking potential is all about. (p. 32)

Fullan presently serves as a special advisor to the Premier of Ontario and the Minister of Education. In collaboration with him, the Ontario government is taking a new approach to school improvement that focuses on alignment. Districts now have greater ability to align resources and strategies in ways that allow teachers to be successful. "Unlocking Potential For Learning—Effective District-Wide Strategies to Raise Student Achievement in Literacy and Numeracy," a report written by Carol Campbell and Michael Fullan (2006), stated that Ontario has recognized that "sustained improvement depends on schools, districts, and provinces adopting an aligned approach that builds the capacity of teachers, school leaders, boards, district leaders, parents, and community allies" (p. 3).

Dealing With Rocks and Hard Places

Throughout the book, we have referred to two kinds of leadership challenges: technical and adaptive. Technical challenges are those that can be solved through the knowledge of experts or senior authorities. Adaptive challenges, on the other hand, must be solved by the people who are part of them. Adaptive leadership is required.

Adaptive leadership tells people what they need to hear rather than what they want to hear, and in the process is likely to evoke considerable emotion as people realize the changes they are being asked to make and the losses they are being asked to sustain in the process. Adaptive leadership mobilizes schools, families, and communities to deal with difficult issues they might prefer to sweep under the rug. It works to close the gap between stated values and actual behaviors because if we are truly committed to learning by all, we must be prepared to do whatever it takes to make it happen. It is likely to mean changes to teaching and assessment practice, to reporting practice, and to familiar structures and policies. Adaptive leadership is complex and difficult.

Sustainability of adaptive leadership is a priority in districts that are aligned. Such leadership involves planning and preparing for succession on an ongoing basis. Succession planning goes beyond grooming administrative successors to distributing leadership throughout the entire professional community so that the productive work being done will continue when existing leaders move on. Hargreaves and Fink (2004) noted that "leadership can not be left to individuals, however talented or dedicated they are. If we want change to matter, to spread, and to last, then the systems in which leaders do their work must make sustainability a priority" (p. 13).

As Fullan (2005) has said, "the work of sustainability is . . . very hard to do, with lots of backward steps along the way" (p. 102). Heifetz and Linsky (2004) concurred that "leading meaningful change in education takes courage, commitment and political savvy" (p. 33). They suggested that political savvy involves building networks for solving problems and presented five essential aspects of political thinking that are helpful in exercising adaptive leadership:

1. **Don't do it alone.** Find people to work with. It may be tempting to go it alone because working with others requires more time and other viewpoints to consider. By enlisting partners, however, political power is built, and thinking is enriched through collaboration.

2. **Keep the opposition close.** Effective leadership involves working as closely with opponents as with supporters. It is necessary to understand the perspectives of those who oppose new initiatives, to know which people have the most to lose, which are sitting on the fence, and which are resisting merely because they don't want their lives disrupted and their futures made uncertain.

3. **Acknowledge their loss.** When people are asked to leave behind something they have done or believed in for many years, they will experience loss even if they understand and value the reason for making the change. The losses must be acknowledged and respected.

4. **Accept casualties.** People who simply cannot or will not go along with the change that is required will become casualties. Leaders must choose between keeping those people and making progress. Acceptance of losses sends a clear message about a leader's courage and commitment to seeing through the change.

5. **Accept responsibility for your piece of the mess.** It behooves leaders to identify personal behaviors or values that could impede progress and accept responsibility for their own contributions to challenges being addressed. It is important to avoid laying blame on others. It is much more powerful to accept responsibility and face the problem together. (Heifetz & Linsky, 2004)

A district aligned around learning for all focuses on adaptive leadership in support of the entire community. An aligned district provides its schools with structures, assistance, and opportunities for getting better both individually and with each other. In such districts, the essential aspects of political thinking are evident and reflected in existing working structures and relationships. It is not easy, but it is worth it.

What the Lesson Teaches Us

- Districts with cultures that are positive, supportive, and forward-looking are conducive to improving school and student success throughout the system.

- Plans and actions to bring about change may be perceived by some as threats.

- Misalignment robs a district of energy and commitment.

- Aligned districts are characterized by:

  ◊ Clearly stated nonnegotiable beliefs that channel energy and effort

  ◊ Common direction and collective purpose; everyone has a responsibility for changing the larger educational context for the better.

  ◊ Focus on teaching and learning for both adults and students

  ◊ Structures and roles that support the mission of learning by all

  ◊ Resource allocation in the service of teaching and learning

  ◊ Lateral networking experiences that engage educators in all roles in cross-school collaboration both within the district and beyond

  ◊ Extensive two-way communication between stakeholders that deepens shared ownership and commitment

  ◊ Continuous reflection and refinement of structures and approaches through systematic inquiry that invites feedback and input from stakeholders

  ◊ Shared leadership with teams of people creating and implementing a clear, coherent strategy for teaching and learning

  ◊ Leadership that comes from many places within the system

- Technical challenges can be addressed by calling upon technical experts. Adaptive challenges, on the other hand, can only be addressed by the people who are involved within the context in which they occur.

- Adaptive leadership focused on instruction is the key to successful alignment.

- Adaptive leadership:

  ◊ Does what is required to ensure that the organization's purpose, vision, and values are known; that structures and processes are in place to support them; and that people have opportunities to take action to make a difference

  ◊ Often involves challenging people to live up to their word—to close the gap between espoused values and actual behavior

  ◊ Ensures that people hear what they *need* to hear rather that what they *want* to hear

  ◊ Recognizes that "resistance comes naturally; learning complicated things in a group setting does not" (Fullan, 2005, p. 101)

  ◊ Takes courage, commitment, and political savvy

  ◊ Ensures that external partnerships are aligned with the system's goals

- Alignment between schools, districts, and the province or state is critical if school improvement is to be sustained. District administrators are the key to facilitating the bottom-up and top-down communication and shared understanding that are critical for school and student success.

Lessons Lived: A Story From the Real World

Schools in districts that are aligned have the advantage of working toward a clearly articulated overall vision and benefiting from support that is provided by senior administrators and trustees. The story that follows is an example of strong central administration and alignment practices that are having a significant impact on all of the schools in the district.

Upper Canada District School Board

Upper Canada District School Board is located in Eastern Ontario. It stretches along the St. Lawrence River and encompasses a large geographical area (12,132 km) bordering the province of Quebec in the east, Ottawa—the Canadian capital—on the north, and the Limestone School District and Kingston on the west. The central administrative office is located in

Brockville, Ontario. Cornwall is the largest city in the district, with a population of 45,965. The district budget is approaching 300 million dollars.

The district has 99 schools divided into four regions. The director of education is the CEO of the district, and each region has a superintendent of education. The schools have an enrollment of approximately 20,000 elementary students in 75 schools and 14,000 secondary students in 24 schools. About 17% of the students receive special education assistance. There are approximately 1,900 teachers and 500 paraprofessionals. Most of the district is rural, with numerous small towns and villages. Maintaining community schools is an ongoing challenge for the district. Upper Canada District was established through the amalgamation of four smaller districts in 1998. The amalgamation took a great deal of energy out of the system. Issues such as staff placement, compensation, and conditions of employment had to be addressed. Perhaps the biggest challenge was the creation of a new district culture.

Creating a New District

The focus shifted from past history to future success when David Thomas was appointed director of education and CEO in 2004. David had broad experience in education, having worked in the same capacity as superintendent of schools in the Peel Board, just west of Toronto. He also had a strong background in athletics both as a coach and as a lacrosse and hockey player. When he came to Upper Canada, he combined his knowledge of school administration, coaching, and teamwork to create a personal model of leadership that has made this one of the premier districts in the province.

When David began in Upper Canada, he, along with his 12-member director's council, and the Board realized that the district needed a structure that would provide a common way of seeing its future. They knew that it would take a minimum of 5 to 7 years to create the culture they envisioned. As part of his entry plan, David and members of his team conducted a 100 x 100 review, during which they met with 100 people over 100 days to gather critical evidence about existing structures and practices that would inform their understanding of the Board and assist with future planning. The people interviewed were representative of all positions and geographical locations in the district.

When the review was completed, David worked with his team to analyze the information that had been gathered and create a framework within which four distinct categories were identified: **C**ommunication, **R**esources, **E**ducational programs, and **W**ellness. CREW is the acronym that was adopted to provide the structure for strategic planning over the next 15 years. Four over-arching planning goals were articulated:

1. A 90% graduation rate by 2020

2. Success for all students (Michelangelo Project)

3. Student and staff wellness

4. Recognition as the voice for small high schools

Leadership for CREW was distributed throughout the district with the creation of project teams in each of the four areas. The projects had clearly defined objectives and outcomes, and the teams were comprised of people from central office and the field. One person, usually a member of the director's council, served as the designated chair or project sponsor.

An internal planning document, the *CREW Strategic Handbook,* articulated the first of a 3-year plan. It was distributed to trustees and all system leaders. Two leadership days were held in August 2004 to launch the plan for the upcoming school year. The plan detailed 54 projects distributed among the four CREW areas. A CREW strategic review team would analyze the progress made on the projects toward the end of the year. The *CREW Strategic Handbook* for the next year would be developed based on their findings.

David Thomas, in his director's message for the 2004–05 handbook, indicated that the CREW strategic plan would be a "chance to shake off the dust, to be inspired again not only to do better, but to meet our potential to be the board by which others are measured, to bring to our work the same sense of enthusiasm, hope and promise each one of us felt the first day we walked into class as a teacher." He went on to say that "CREW isn't just an acronym, it's the philosophy I want this board to adopt—a philosophy of working together as a team to overcome adversity and paddle towards success. Like the crew of a racing canoe we must work in harmony, work as a crew to overcome the whitewater we may face, and most of all keep our eye on the finish line—always striving to be world class."

It is not unusual for school districts to establish a strategic plan and lay out a number of programs and strategies. Probably every district in North

America has a strategic plan somewhere on a shelf. What makes the Upper Canada process different is that its plan is a living document that is consistently monitored and embedded into daily practice. Each year, revisions are introduced based on learning from the year before.

2004–05 CREW Projects

1. Communications. Upper Canada undertook 20 projects in the communications area with the goal of ensuring purposeful, ongoing, open exchanges of ideas, sharing of information, and an awareness of decisions. The following list includes some of the projects:

- Train principals in the area of human resource management to decrease energy lost in labor and human rights issues.

- Monitor the impact of school success plans using Dashboard Metrics, a monitoring system to provide information about progress and next steps.

- Improve information technology service so that it is transparent, useful, and reliable.

- Provide clearly stated information regarding special education mandates.

- Create a brand for each school that is aligned with professional learning community principles.

- Align the roles of principals and vice principals with CREW, and ensure that the promotion process identifies individuals who will make a positive contribution.

2. Resources. There were 14 projects in the resources area with the goal of allocating people and resources in a transparent, effective, and fair manner that meets the needs of their diverse community. Examples of the projects are:

- Eliminate non–value–added work.

- Allocate school resources to support published success plans.

- Monitor the quality of central services to ensure they are supporting school success.

- Encourage data-based planning throughout the system by ensuring data are available and meaningful.

- Ensure that the budget process places financial resources where they are needed and will be used most effectively.

- Establish research practices that will identify classroom practices that positively impact student performance, and make this information available throughout the system.

- Reorganize the adult and continuing education programs so they better serve student needs and maximize the revenue stream to the district.

- Realign special education services to gain the maximum student benefit from staff.

- Decentralize school staffing so that families of schools can determine where staff can be best placed to serve schools.

3. Education. Upper Canada initiated 12 education projects to lead in the initiation, development, and promotion of world-class education programs and services. Some of the projects included are:

- Develop online programs that will ensure that small high schools can offer a full menu of courses to all students.

- Identify schools that have failed to meet provincial expectations for 3 years, and introduce specific strategies that will raise their performance by at least 5%.

- Implement effective professional learning community strategies to support school and system improvement.

- Develop model schools to meet the diverse needs of the district communities.

- Develop and implement a "school review model" that will allow for the collection and sharing of meaningful data as well as the designation of exemplary programs that should be implemented in other schools.

- Increase leadership capacity by developing programs to nurture, grow, and renew leadership at the school level.

- Create and implement programs that will ensure all graduating grade 12 students will achieve at the required provincial standard for literacy.

4. Wellness. There were eight wellness projects intended to nurture a respectful, inclusive, and safe community where people listen and respond. Some examples of wellness projects are:

- Implement quality daily physical education.

- Embed character education in all curricula.

- Introduce a program to regularly recognize those who go the extra mile.

- Create career paths for talented educators to ensure retention and have a positive impact on morale.

Outcomes and Next Steps

At the end of the 2004–05 year, 11 of the 54 original projects had met their target with significant positive results. Based on the work of the strategic review team, *CREW Strategic Handbook 1.1* was developed for the 2005–06 year. Eighteen new projects were added to address provincial mandates or discoveries that were made during the implementation of the original CREW document. *CREW Strategic Handbook 1.2* was created for 2006–07 and by the end of that school year, an amazing 32 CREW projects had met their targets. Each year at leadership days in August, the handbook was distributed to trustees and all system leaders as a reference for the year ahead.

Longitudinal data for provincial assessments in grades 3, 6, 9, and 10 over the course of the first 3-year phase of CREW strategic planning show that significant gains were made as a result of its efforts.

Table 9-1: Percentage of Students Achieving Provincial Standards on the EQAO Assessments

Subject Area	2003–04	2004–05	2005–06	2006–07
Grade 3 Reading	54	60	62	59
Grade 3 Writing	52	58	59	60
Grade 3 Math	66	70	72	69
Grade 6 Reading	52	63	63	60
Grade 6 Writing	45	56	55	51
Grade 6 Math	48	59	61	58
Grade 9 Academic Math	67	65	66	69
Grade 9 Applied Math	29	28	39	43
Grade 10 OSSLT ((Ontario Secondary School Literacy Test)	75	82	84	84

2005–06 marked the end of Phase 1, the first 3 years of Upper Canada's 15-year voyage to become the board by which others are measured. Phase 2, the next 3-year period (2007–2010), was ready to be launched.

Staying the Course. The end of Phase 1 marked 1,000 days since the introduction of CREW, so the decision was made to conduct a 1,000 x 1,000 review between April and June 2007, to gather perspective on the goals and projects identified in Phase 1. One thousand people were interviewed regarding progress made over the 1,000 days since the introduction of CREW. Staff representing all roles in Upper Canada were interviewed, as well as students, parents, and members of the community. The review was intended to assist with planning for the second 3-year phase of the 15-year CREW strategic plan. It addressed three issues: Are we on the right track? What gaps need to be overcome? How should we proceed from here?

Three separate interview methods were used to ensure proficient and impartial results:

1. Nancy Hanna, principal of School Success Planning, conducted lead interviews, overseen by a 21-member survey team consisting of central office staff and school-based administrators.

2. Two outside consultants conducted external interviews.

3. Director and CEO David Thomas conducted focus group interviews.

Also in preparation for Phase 2, the Board revisited its original belief, vision, and mission statements with the intention of developing operational guidelines that would support alignment between the system plan and individual school plans.

The UCDSB Mission Statement: We prepare all students for a successful life.

The UCDSB Vision: Creating Futures, Leading and Learning for All

The UCDSB Credo/Virtues: Character always! Caring, Fairness, Honesty, Empathy, Responsibility, Perseverance, Respect, Resilience

The UCDSB Philosophy: Every Student *Will* Learn.

The UCDSB Focus: Operational Excellence

During the 1,000 x 1,000 review, the review teams heard that CREW was working well and that it would be important to stay the course in order to consolidate and enrich the work that had been started. When the plan for the 07–08 school year was articulated in *CREW Strategic Handbook 2.0*, it was given the subtitle "Staying the Course." For the 08–09 school year, the *Crew Strategic Handbook 2.1* is subtitled "Operational Excellence."

Supporting Alignment. To coincide with the launch of phase 2 of CREW, Nancy Hanna, principal of School Success Planning, compiled the *Continuous System Success* framework, a binder that is a compendium of materials to support system leaders in aligning their school success plans with the system plan. In it, the Upper Canada *journey and action pillars of success* have been identified as innovation, collaboration, and accountability.

Innovation. Upper Canada developed a number of innovations to guide and support all schools in the district.

- School Culture Scan: The School Culture Scan, an anonymous survey for teachers and administrators, is based on the correlates of effective schools. It is administered every 6–8 months. Teachers are involved in the collection and tabulation of culture scan results. The results are used for school improvement planning. The focus areas of the School Culture Scan are as follows—

  ◊ A positive, safe school culture and climate

  ◊ Balanced and responsive assessment

  ◊ High expectations for success

  ◊ A viable curriculum

  ◊ Collegiality and professionalism

  ◊ Strong and focused leadership

  ◊ Clearly stated goals and direction

  ◊ Positive parent and community relations

- Strategy Room: The results of each school's culture scan, along with provincial and school-based achievement results, are posted in the strategy room at central office for all to see. Periodically, the administrators of each high school and its feeder schools meet in the strategy room with the senior administrators. There they collectively review and analyze their school success plans with a view to identifying strategies for aligning their efforts in order to work together as they move forward.

- Building Capacity: The senior administration of Upper Canada District realizes that effective leadership is the vehicle for change and improvement. They make it a priority to work with those currently in leadership roles and those aspiring to leadership positions. The leadership training theme for Phase 1 of CREW was *Embracing Change Moving Forward* (2004–2007). The Phase 2 theme is *Staying the Course* (2007–2010). Leadership modules have been created to develop capacity in these areas:

  ◊ P.O.W.E.R.

    P—Clearly defining the *problem* and situation.

    O—Determining who *owns* the problem.

    W—Answering *what, when,* and *who?*

    E—*Evaluating* issues and determining potential remedies and responses.

    R—*Remedy, response, review, revisit*

  ◊ Crucial Conversations

  ◊ Tag the Top! High Performance Teams in Education

  ◊ H 2 0—Hope, Happiness, and Opportunity

- The Michelangelo Project: Inspired by sculptor Michelangelo, this is a conceptual framework to ensure that each student reaches his or her true potential. A *Michelangelo student* is one who at any time is at risk to not graduate or reach his or her true pathway. The goal of the Michelangelo project is to establish and maintain a tracking system to support schools in their efforts to provide personalized educational planning for students.

> Inside every block of marble dwells a beautiful statue; one need only remove the excess material to reveal the work of art inside.

> I saw the angel in the marble and carved until I set him free.

> —Michelangelo

Collaboration. Upper Canada developed three programs to support and facilitate authentic collaboration that would lead to action and increased student success.

- Learning Conversations: This program was launched during the 2006–07 school year to provide school-based professional learning teams with focused opportunities to engage in collaboration and meaningful conversations for student-centered improvement planning. Twenty-six schools were involved in the first year, and the number had expanded to 34 in 2007–2008. Specific skills and strategies were taught to help the schools to learn from each other and build capacity for authentic collaboration. This program will continue into the future.

- Action Research: During the 2005–06 school year, four schools were selected to pilot this 3-year project. Phase 1 focused on data compilation and analysis.

  Phase 2 (2006–07) involved teaching the skills of action research to explore the following—

  ◊ How provincial test scores can be linked with report-card data to predict and measure student success

  ◊ How this data could be used to support school improvement planning

  Phase 3 (2007–08) built on the momentum from Phase 2 to identify action research projects and align them with school success plans. This model of embedded professional development is of interest to increasingly greater numbers of Upper Canada schools.

- Small High Schools Summit: Being a predominantly rural district, Upper Canada has many small high schools that face unique programming challenges because of their size. Each year the district hosts a 3-day conference to celebrate best practices and the success of small high schools in the region.

- The Wellness Program: In collaboration with Dr. Linda Duxbury, one of Canada's leading workplace health researchers, staff from the Upper Canada human resources department have designed programs to improve employee wellness. Other wellness initiatives include Quality Daily Physical Education, volunteer recognition programs, and program support for character education.

Accountability. Upper Canada introduced a new school success planning process that aligns the accountability strategies of the school and district with those of the province.

- School Success Plans: Each school is required to create a plan to improve using the four elements of CREW. The plans include strategies for improving *communication* with students, parents, and staff; using *resources* to improve student learning outcomes; identifying the *educational* approaches that will be used to impact student success; and ensuring the health and *wellness* of students, staff, and the community.

  Each of the four sections of the School Success Plan has an action team and chair to take the lead on behalf of the school. The team identifies objectives, the specific strategies that they will employ to reach their objectives, and the data they will use to measure success.

- School Audit: The district has appointed an alignment and accountability officer to ensure that the School Success Plan process is being followed and successfully implemented. An audit process has been developed and an audit team assigned to each school. The audit team involves school staff as well as the area superintendent and other members of the director's council. The audit takes place over a period of 3–5 months and is very structured, so that there are no surprises. The final stage of the audit is a sign-off by the director indicating approval of the school's performance.

- School Data Profile: Using Dashboard Metrics, a web-based data warehouse for data collection and analysis used by school administrators, schools create school profiles that provide critical evidence for school success planning. School data profiles provide information on numerous aspects of the school such as student demographics, discipline information, cocurricular activities, provincial achievement scores, credits gained and lost, graduation rates, and staff development.

- CREW Reflective Audit: As part of the School Success Plan review, school administrators and school teams evaluate themselves on the following criteria:

  ◊ Shared mission, vision, values, and credo

  ◊ Systematic methods of communicating with all stakeholders

◊ Budget support for the strategic plan

◊ Budget being accurately maintained

◊ Information for decision-making

◊ Information management

◊ System wellness data

◊ Workplace wellness data

The Last Word

Wayne Hulley, one of the authors of this book, was contracted as an external consultant to the Upper Canada District School Board in May 2007. As part of his work with the district, he visited schools and attended meetings to assess the impact of the planning and implementation that have arisen from CREW. He was impressed by the enthusiasm he felt in the schools and in the central office as well as the results of the CREW initiative. Although the Upper Canada District School Board created a large number of programs, the system was never overwhelmed because the programs were aligned with the four components of the CREW strategic initiatives. The projects had a clear focus, specific objectives, and a declared method for evaluating results. As a result, the staff of Upper Canada can truly say that learning by all is becoming a reality in their district. They are making a difference.

Summary

School improvement happens in schools one classroom at a time. It is not an easy process, but research tells us that instructional leadership at the district level will help to address challenges at the school level. The elements for district success include:

• Solid alignment of district policies, procedures, and strategies

• Clearly articulated mission, vision, and values

• High expectations for improvement

• Support for learning

Successful districts achieve exciting results for all schools, their students, their parents, and the community at large.

10

Looking to the Future With Hope

Douglas Reeves (2006) contended that education is "awash in mythology" that has a "tinge of truth or a whisper of research" that seems to give it credibility but, in fact, does not provide enough evidence to "sustain scrutiny" (p. 91). Myths die in the face of evidence, observation, and experience to contradict them. Reeves encouraged us to confront the myths that serve as barriers to doing the real work to improve our schools and achieve success for all. He identified (and dispelled) five such myths.

Myth #1: People are happy doing what they are doing now. Teachers in unsuccessful schools would rather continue to be unsuccessful than engage in alternative practices that might lead to improved student success.

In fact, people are miserable when they do not feel successful in their personal and professional lives. They are most motivated by work that is meaningful and by a sense that their personal efforts make a difference.

Myth #2: People resist change because of irrational fear. In fact, many resist change because previous unsuccessful change initiatives have left them cynical and suspicious.

Myth #3: You can't make significant changes until you get buy-in from everybody. In fact, the cycle of organizational improvement is not "vision, buy-in, action" but rather "vision, action, buy-in and more action." Behavior precedes belief. If you wait for people to have buy-in, be happy, or change belief systems, then change will never happen.

Myth #4: You must have perfect research to support a proposed change. In fact, perfect research does not exist. The quality model that prevails throughout successful organizations is not waiting for perfection but rather "Try it, test it, improve it."

Myth #5: The risk of change is so great that you must wait until you have things perfectly organized before implementing change efforts. In fact, change never gets easier; it's never convenient, universally popular, without opposition, or risk free. (Reeves, 2006, p. 95)

Every day, schools choose between getting by or getting better. Schools that choose to get better engage in deliberate planning to improve, and in doing so embark on a process that is both challenging and invigorating. The commitment to getting better is really a commitment to shifting the culture of the school to make learning by all a reality.

This belief is central to all of the writing in this book—it is also what we have heard from the teachers and principals with whom we worked—getting by is easy, getting better is not—but it is worth doing whatever it takes to make a difference for kids.

You have read that leadership for getting better is critical, and that to have the greatest power, it must be distributed among all staff members. Formal leadership is the driving force for building capacity and empowering others to come to the fore. Without formal leadership, the chances of informal leadership emerging are limited. Without strong informal leadership, improvement initiatives will not be sustained, and schools will not get better. In the absence of strong shared leadership, some staff have no incentive to do anything but hunker down and wait for the current administration to go away so that they can continue to do openly what they've always done. Strong leadership is improvisational, responsive, creative, and focused. It requires courage, commitment, and passion. Getting better is contingent on such leadership.

> ▶ It is not easy—but it is worth it for the sake of the children and youth with whom we work.

The seven correlates of effective schools have withstood the test of time and are stronger than ever in the second generation. They serve as markers to guide improvement efforts. In schools where learning by all is a reality, the correlates work in concert and are interdependent. All seven are consistently present and powerfully demonstrated.

Schools that get better focus on the second-generation correlates and understand that our current educational mission is not just high literacy and numeracy scores. It is also about educating students to understand themselves as learners and how to learn effectively. Fundamental skills are important; however, self-management and teamwork skills are equally important. Schools that are getting better focus their attention on preparing students for their futures as citizens of the world.

After reflecting on what we have learned since writing *Harbors of Hope* (Hulley & Dier, 2005), what we have learned in writing this book, and what we have learned through our work with schools in the real world, we present a checklist for getting better, not just getting by, in appendix C (page 213). We also identify the following essential learnings about effective schools in our diverse and ever-changing world:

- The school must be all (and only) about learning—student learning and adult learning.

- Ongoing professional development and growth are not optional.

- Schools that are getting better concentrate on academics, but go beyond to include consideration of all aspects of student development for their future in the adult world.

- When schools understand and rely on the seven correlates of effective schools to guide their improvement work, they will get better.

- Succinctly stated, the second generation of correlates tells us—

  ◊ Without a clearly articulated, focused mission that is shared by all, improvement efforts will flounder.

  ◊ Students and adults cannot focus and take the risks required to learn if the school environment is not safe and orderly.

  ◊ Measurement is critical. It is as important to monitor improvement efforts frequently as it is to monitor student growth and achievement frequently.

  Two questions provide incentive for using critical evidence:

  1. How can we determine if our efforts are making a difference if we do not know where we started?

  2. Why would we bother measuring progress if we are not going to use the information to adjust our practice?

  ◊ In-flight correction goes with the territory.

◊ A climate of high expectations for both students and staff is essential.

◊ High expectations are neither fair nor achievable without adequate opportunity to learn and time on task.

◊ Strong relationships between the school, home, and community make it possible to do more to enhance both school and student success. This is true for students *and* teachers.

◊ Effective instructional leadership makes collaboration a priority and embeds it in the culture. Instructional leadership must be strong at both the school and district levels to promote and support overall improvement.

◊ Strong formal instructional leadership facilitates the growth of leadership capacity throughout the school and the district.

Our thinking is framed within a lexicon of hope—and we distinguish between hope and wishful thinking. *Hope* is proactive and tenacious, resulting in doing whatever it takes to make success for all a reality, regardless of how many in-flight corrections are required. *Wishful thinking,* on the other hand, is passive and often serves to alleviate feelings of guilt for not being proactive.

In *Harbors of Hope,* we defined *hope* as "a form of optimism that often seems unwarranted. . . . in the face of incredible odds. It is the incentive that keeps people keeping on" (Hulley & Dier, 2005, p. 3). In schools, hope is the belief that all students can learn. It is hope that inspires educators to make that happen. It prevents panic and discouragement when success seems out of reach and keeps teachers searching for strategies and resources that will benefit all students. Hope is a powerful emotion that is essential to sustaining the efforts of both students and staff. When adults join forces to collaborate on behalf of children and youth, the results can be dramatic.

The schools and districts featured in this book have generously shared their experiences with moving beyond getting by to getting better. As authors, we have been privileged to work with and learn from them, and we appreciate the opportunity to share their stories with our readers. We hope that you will find the information in this book beneficial, and we wish you well in making the choice between getting by or getting better.

Appendices

A

Rubric for Reviewing School Information

Benchmark: Data Validate Improved Student Achievement

4 School is able to provide solid, longitudinal provincial and school or classroom-based data that show significant overall improved student achievement in at least two disciplines, as well as in areas such as course completion and attendance over a period of 2–3 years.

3 School is able to provide longitudinal provincial data and school or classroom-based data that show some improvement in student achievement in one discipline, as well as course completion and attendance over a period of at least 2 years.

2 School is beginning to use data; however, results are still sketchy and understanding about how to use data is just developing.

1 School is not using data effectively. Improved student achievement is not validated by data.

Benchmark: A Collaborative Culture Is Evident

4 Much evidence is given to illustrate that staff works collaboratively in teams as well as at the whole-school level. Business at this school is conducted in a spirit of authentic collaboration, acknowledging the pitfalls and challenges that accompany these kinds of working relationships. Collaboration is embedded in the school's culture.

3 Collaboration is valued, and some evidence exists to illustrate that staff is working to develop authentic collaborative working relationships. There are some strong collaborative teams in the school. The culture is increasingly collaborative.

2 Collaborative working relationships are beginning to be developed. The will seems to be present; however, the how-tos are missing. Collaboration is a sketchy, but emerging, concept at the school.

1 The language of collaboration is being used, but the talk is not being walked. They only *think* they get it.

Benchmark: Teacher Leadership Is Evident

4 Leadership is shared among staff members, regardless of their individual positions. Administrators validate teacher leadership and actively involve teachers in the Planning for School and Student Success Process. The school administrators are conscientious about providing opportunities and training to develop leadership capacity in teachers. Shared leadership is an accepted way of working at this school, and relationships reflect that.

3 There is evidence of administrative effort to share or distribute leadership at the school. There is also evidence of teacher willingness to assume leadership roles with support. Shared leadership is valued, although not entirely understood or fully supported. The culture is beginning to shift in favor of increased teacher leadership capacity.

2 The language of shared leadership is used, and it is said to be valued. While some efforts are made to distribute decision-making and planning capacity, leadership is still firmly ensconced in formal roles (administration and department heads) with a hesitation to "loosen the reins" and give up control.

1 The concept of shared and distributed leadership is either not understood or not valued. Those in formal leadership roles, most particularly, the administration, still think they need to do it all.

Benchmark: Concrete Strategies Related to Improved Student Learning Can Be Identified

4 Numerous strategies have been implemented, and data show they have been significant in the improvement of student learning outcomes. Staff has used data to identify areas of strength and weakness in order to inform their planning efforts. In addition, they have used what is known about high-yield strategies and been proactive about adapting them for their school. School improvement planning has been purposeful and proactive. Plans are strategic, monitored regularly, and evaluated based on observable evidence. Student achievement is the number-one priority.

3 Planning has resulted in identifying and implementing strategies designed to improve student learning outcomes. Data are being used to inform the planning, and staff members are working diligently to implement the plans they have developed. Implementation of strategies, use of data, and monitoring could be more effective, and the plan could be more detailed and focused. It is unclear if student achievement is really the number-one priority or if other things are interfering.

2 While staff is working hard, the data that would indicate improvement are sketchy, making it difficult to determine whether the hard work is really making a difference. There is a lot of good talk, but evidence of improved achievement is lacking.

1 Staff is planning to plan. Many plans exist, but there is no evidence of proactive work aimed at improved student achievement or any means of measuring it.

B

Schools That Contributed to
Getting By or Getting Better

This appendix lists the schools that responded to our request for information from the field. We were pleased that so many schools were willing to work with us, and it was difficult to narrow the field in order to make the amount of information manageable. Although we have highlighted 14 schools, our findings reflect the work of all of the schools listed in Table A-1, because they have much in common. Schools that are getting better do similar things.

Table A-1: Participating Schools

School	Principal	Division/District
Bloordale Middle School	Nick Tran	Toronto District School Board
Briarcrest Junior School	Jacqueline Goh	Toronto District School Board
Busby School	Michelle Webb	Pembina Hills Regional Division
* Carlton Comprehensive High School	Dawn Kilmer	Saskatchewan Rivers School Division
Central School	Jody Rutherford	Grasslands Regional Division
Chateauguay Valley Regional H.S.	Patricia Peter	New Frontiers School Board
* Chimo Elementary School	Laurie McCabe	Upper Canada District School Board
* C.J. Schurter School	Robyn Ord-Boisvert	High Prairie School Division
Early Literacy Project	Maureen Taylor	Saskatchewan Rivers School Division
Eastdale Elementary School	Janice Robertshaw	Hamilton Wentworth District SB
* École Charleswood School	Iain Riffel	Pembina Trails School Division
George Symes Community School	Margaret McKenzie	Toronto District School Board
* G.L. Roberts Collegiate and Voc. Inst.	Ian Skinner	Durham District School Board
Glendale Secondary School	John Whitwell	Hamilton Wentworth District SB
Griffin Park School	Mark Crozier	Grasslands Regional Division
* Harry Sayers Elementary School	Susan Antak	Abbotsford School District

School	Principal	Division/District
* Holy Trinity Catholic High School	John Burroughs	Brant Haldimand Norfolk Catholic DSB
Horse Hill School	Sheila Tingley	Edmonton Public School Board
* Khowhemun Elementary School	Charlie Coleman	Cowichan Valley School District
Kingsford-Smith Elementary School	Errol Joe	Vancouver School Board
Kinistino School	Tom Hazzard	Saskatchewan Rivers School Division
Lakeshore Collegiate Institute	Beth Butcher	Toronto District School Board
Lord Kitchener Elementary School	Kathy O'Sullivan	Vancouver School Board
Merrickville Public School	Ray Westendorp	Upper Canada District School Board
Olds High School	Tom Christensen	Chinook's Edge School Division
* Pierre Elliott Trudeau Elementary School	Marian Lothian	Western Quebec School Board
Princess Margaret Junior School	Carter Logan	Toronto District School Board
R. A. Riddell Elementary School	Wes Hahn	Hamilton Wentworth District SB
Lord Roberts Elementary School	Val Coopersmith	Vancouver School Board
* Rockcliffe Middle School	Kevin Battaglia	Toronto District School Board
Seneca School	Margaret Lunnie	Toronto District School Board
* Sir John A. Macdonald Secondary School	Michael Rehill	Hamilton Wentworth District SB
Sir Winston Churchill Secondary School	Peter Joshua	Hamilton Wentworth District SB
* Somerset and District Elementary School	Heather Morse	Annapolis Valley Regional SB
System Alternative Ed. Programs	Dale Pyke	Hamilton Wentworth District SB
Tilley School Programs	Szandra Muschiol	Grasslands Regional Division
Tri-School Initiative: Blessed Sacrament School St. Anthony Daniel Catholic School St. Theresa School	Don Backus Jennifer Rudyk Leslie Telfer	Brant Haldimand Norfolk Catholic DSB
* Valley Farm Public School	Silvia Peterson	Durham District School Board
* Vancouver Technical Secondary School	David Derpak	Vancouver School Board
Vincent Massey Public School	Carol Pattendon	Durham District School Board
West Glen Junior School	Sue Bois	Toronto District School Board
Westgrove Elementary School	Susan Schmidt	Pembina Trails School Division
Westlock Elementary School	Terry Anderson	Pembina Hills Regional Division

* Indicates the schools whose stories are told in the body of this book

C

Getting Better, Not Just Getting By: A Structured Plan to Improve

Schools that get better are all traveling on a multilane superhighway. Some schools are traveling faster than others, but they all know where they are going. Their destination is a Harbor of Hope, where learning by all is a reality. If your school plans to take the journey, you will need a map that will get you there in the most efficient way possible. What follows is a TripTik that ensures you will not get lost on the side roads. Although the school planning process is never linear, it is wise to plan sequentially so that you can mark your arrival at critical checkpoints along the journey. We suggest that your staff use this TripTik to focus your discussions, energy, and actions.

1. **The school creates or renews its values, vision, and mission (purpose) statements.**

   You need to be clear on where you want to go and what it will look like when you arrive. You should include as many of your passengers (stakeholders) as possible in making the travel plans because they will need to understand the destination and the route you intend to follow.

2. **Critical evidence is gathered around the things that matter to the school.**

   You would not begin a major trip without a complete check of your vehicle. You would also have the necessary maintenance done before you start the trip.

   To prepare for the school improvement journey, identify the needs of your students and what steps need to be taken to ensure their success on the journey of life. The critical evidence that guides the journey should include data on achievement, attendance, attitudes, and behavior.

3. **The critical evidence is organized and analyzed to determine areas of strength and those needing improvement.**

Some maintenance items on your vehicle are more critical than others. Based on your budget, you would repair those things that have the greatest potential to enable you to complete the trip successfully. To have the repairs done, you would seek expert technicians on whom you could rely to do the job.

In school improvement, you must prioritize student needs and work on those that are most important first. This prioritizing is best done by experts. In schools, the experts are the staff working most closely with the students.

4. **The staff forms professional learning communities (PLCs).**

In servicing your vehicle, you would want to know that the person fixing your air conditioner malfunction knows how air conditioners work.

In school improvement, the expert groups are collaborative teams, working as a professional learning community (PLC). These teams share responsibility for a group of students and are in the best position to make judgments and offer solutions. Some issues that center on safe and orderly environments and home-school relations are best dealt with by the whole staff. Other issues that center on high expectations for success, opportunity to learn, and time on task are best addressed by subject-area or grade-level teaching teams.

5. **SMART goals are established based on the collected and analyzed critical evidence.**

In maintaining your automobile, the goals are often established around a computer printout presented by the technician who explains the priority of repairs, the approximate cost, and the expected time of completion.

In schools, the collaborative team needs to establish clearly stated goals, ideally in the SMART format: specific, measurable, attainable, results-focused, and time-bound.

6. **The teams explore high-yield strategies that could move them in the direction of positively impacting the goal.**

In the automobile maintenance shop, the technicians would begin to organize the customized tools and monitoring equipment necessary to complete the repairs.

School teams explore strategies, programs, and processes that might be most helpful in reaching the SMART goals. The actions that hold the most promise in reaching the goals are termed *high-yield* strategies.

7. The PLC teams create an action plan for the goal.

The maintenance experts in the shop would begin their work methodically. They would know which parts need to be removed first and which parts are fragile and need special care. Considering all the details, they would take action on the plan to improve the performance of your automobile.

PLC teams create a written plan to improve. The plan includes the SMART goal and a clear statement of the high-yield strategies or actions to be taken.

8. The individualized action plans are organized into a school improvement plan.

The individual actions of the various technicians working on your vehicle lead to the overall quality of the repair.

In schools, the action plans of the various PLC teams are organized into the school plan to improve.

9. The plans must be monitored regularly so adjustments can be made if progress is not being made.

Reputable automobile repair shops usually have a supervisor who monitors the work of the technicians and gives advice as needed. Sometimes it is necessary to refer to a manual or perhaps phone an expert at the head office. If other problems are discovered during the repair, the shop contacts the customer and seeks approval to deal with the needed changes. Regular testing is done as the job progresses to ensure that the repairs are successfully completed.

As collaborative teams work in schools, they often struggle with the changes they are trying to make. They may also discover unanticipated problems as they implement regular formative assessment strategies that clearly show how students are progressing. Teachers can call on other experts in the school, as well as specialists within the district, or they may use technology to search for solutions.

10. PLC teams meet regularly as teams and as a whole staff to report on progress and plan for the future.

When customers arrive to pick up their vehicles, they meet with the maintenance supervisor, who outlines the work that was done and may recommend that certain precautions be taken or future maintenance considered.

Full staff should regularly meet so that PLC teams can share the progress they have made and outline future actions they intend to take. This process keeps all staff aware of the work being done and allows individual teams to adjust their actions to support the work of others.

11. Each year progress is measured, progress is reported, and critical evidence is provided to ensure a continuous improvement mindset.

Before getting into your automobile and setting out on your adventure, the supervisor presents you with a printout of the work completed and the warranty you can expect. This summary can be shared with others or perhaps used to prove mechanical fitness for license renewal. Chances are the printout will recommend some periodic maintenance requirements to ensure the proper functioning of the car.

Toward the end of each year, schools need to summarize where they have been. These reviews are part of regular maintenance for school health and wellness. They should be completed before the conclusion of the school year so that the critical evidence that has been gathered during the year can be considered by the staff in the following year as they begin the 11-step process again. This process supports a continuous improvement mindset in which next year's planning is based on the results from this year.

References

Aboriginal stay-in-school initiative: Native youth advancement with education Hamilton (NYAWEH). Final report for September 2003–2006. Hamilton, Ontario: Hamilton Community Foundation.

Adair, J. (2005). *How to grow leaders: The seven key principles of effective leadership development*. London: Kogan Page Publishing.

Beland, K. (2007). Boosting social and emotional competence. *Educational Leadership, 64*(7), 68–71.

Berkowitz, M., & Bier, M. (2005). Character education: Parents as partners. *Educational Leadership, 64*(1), 64–69.

Bridges, W. (1991). *Managing transitions: Making the most of change*. Reading, MA: Addison-Wesley.

Campbell, C., & Fullan, M. (2006). *Unlocking potential for learning: Effective district-wide strategies to raise student achievement in literacy and numeracy*. Ontario Ministry of Education. Accessed at www.searchontario.gov.on.ca/cgi-bin/e_search_results.pl?offset=0&owner_id=edu&language=en&collection=50800edutcu&query=campbell+fullan on August 7, 2008.

Carolan, J., & Guinn, A. (2007). Differentiation: Lessons from master teachers. *Educational Leadership, 64*(5), 44–47.

Childress, S., Elmore, R., & Grossman, A. (2006, November). How to manage urban school districts. *Harvard Business Review*. Accessed at http://harvardbusinessonline.hbsp.harvard.edu/hbsp/hbr/articles/article.jsp;jsessionid=RW4KPH0QHITKCAKRGWDR5VQBKE0YIISW?ml_action=get-article&articleID=R0611B&ml_page=1&ml_subscriber=true on August 7, 2008.

Collins, J. (2001). *Good to great*. New York: HarperCollins.

Collins, J. (2005). *Good to great and the social sectors*. New York: HarperCollins.

Comer, J. (2005). The rewards of parent participation. *Educational Leadership, 62*(6), 38–42.

Conference Board of Canada. (2000). *Employability skills 2000+*. Accessed at www.conferenceboard.ca/education on August 4, 2008.

Conzemius, A., & O'Neill, J. (2002). *The handbook for SMART school teams*. Bloomington, IN: Solution Tree (formerly National Educational Service).

Covey, S. (1990). *Principle-centered leadership*. New York: Simon & Schuster.

Danielson, C. (2007). The many faces of leadership. *Educational Leadership, 65*(1), 14–19.

Darling-Hammond, L., & Ifill-Lynch, O. (2006). If they'd only do their work! *Educational Leadership, 63*(5), 8–13.

Deming, W. E. (2000). *The new economics for industry, government, education* (2nd ed.). Cambridge, MA: MIT.

DuFour, R., DuFour, R., Eaker, R., & Karhanek, G. (2004). *Whatever it takes: How professional learning communities respond when kids don't learn*. Bloomington, IN: Solution Tree (formerly National Educational Service).

DuFour, R., DuFour, R., Eaker, R., & Many, T. (2006). *Learning by doing: A handbook for professional learning communities at work*. Bloomington, IN: Solution Tree.

Edmonds, R. R. (1982). Programs of school improvement: An overview. *Educational Leadership, 40*(3), 8–11.

Fisher, D., & Frey, N. (2007). *Checking for understanding*. Alexandria, VA: Association for Supervision and Curriculum Development.

Fullan, M. (2001). *Leading in a culture of change*. San Francisco: Jossey-Bass.

Fullan, M. (2005). *Leadership and sustainability*. Thousand Oaks, CA: Corwin.

Fullan, M., Bertani, A., & Quinn, J. (2004). New lessons for district-wide reform. *Educational Leadership, 61*(7), 42–46.

Fullan, M., Cuttress, C., & Kilcher, A. (2005). Eight forces for leaders to change. *Journal of Staff Development, 26*(4), 55–59.

Fullan, M., Hill, P., & Crevola, C. (2006). *Breakthrough*. Thousand Oaks, CA: Corwin.

Fullan, M., & Steigelbauer, S. (1991). *The new meaning of educational change*. New York: Teachers College.

Goleman, D. (1998). *Working with emotional intelligence*. New York: Bantam Books.

Goleman, D., Boyatzis, R., & McKee, A. (2002). *Primal leadership: Realizing the power of emotional intelligence*. Boston: Harvard Business School.

Gurian, M. (2001). *Boys and girls learn differently*. San Francisco: Jossey-Bass.

Guskey, T. R. (2007). The rest of the story. *Educational Leadership, 65*(4), 28–34.

Hall, G., & Hord, S. (1987). *Taking charge of change.* Alexandria, VA: Association for Supervision and Curriculum Development.

Hargreaves, A. (2003). *Teaching in the knowledge society.* New York: Teachers College.

Hargreaves, A., & Fink, D. (2004). The seven principles of sustainable leadership. *Educational Leadership, 61*(7), 9–13.

Heifetz, R., & Linsky, M. (2002). *Leadership on the line: Staying alive through the dangers of leading.* Boston: Harvard Business School.

Heifetz, R., & Linsky, M. (2004). When leadership spells danger. *Educational Leadership, 61*(7), 33–37.

Hulley, W., & Dier, L. (2005). *Harbors of hope: The planning for school and student success process.* Bloomington, IN: Solution Tree (formerly National Educational Service).

Hume, M. (2003, December 2). Vancouver and the violence of Babel. *The Globe and Mail.*

Jerald, C. (2003). Beyond the rock and the hard place. *Educational Leadership, 61*(3), 12–16.

Johnson, S., & Donaldson, M. (2007). Overcoming the obstacles to leadership. *Educational Leadership, 65*(1), 8–13.

Kotter, J. (1996). *Leading change.* Boston: Harvard Business School.

Levine, M. (2007). The essential cognitive backpack. *Educational Leadership, 64*(7), 17–22.

Lezotte, L., & McKee, K. (2002). *Assembly required: A continuous school improvement system.* Okemos, MI: Effective Schools Products, Ltd.

Marzano, R. (2003). *What works in schools: Translating research into action.* Alexandria, VA: Association for Supervision and Curriculum Development.

Mintzberg, H., Ahlstrand, B., & Lampel, J. (1998). *Strategy safari: A guided tour through the wilds of strategic management.* New York: Free Press.

Morrish, R. G. (2000). *With all due respect: Keys for building effective school discipline.* Fonthill, ON: Woodstream Publishing.

Peterson, K. D., & Deal, T. E. (2002). *The shaping school culture fieldbook.* San Francisco: Jossey-Bass.

Reeves, D. (2006). *The learning leader: How to focus school improvement for better results.* Alexandria, VA: Association for Supervision and Curriculum Development.

Rogers, E. (2003). *Diffusion of innovations* (5th ed.). New York: Free Press.

Sadler, D. R. (1989). Formative assessment and the design of instructional systems. *Instructional Science, 18,* 119–144.

Saskatchewan Outdoor and Environmental Education Association and Saskatchewan Education (SOEEA). (1991). *Out to learn: Guidelines and standards for outdoor environmental education* (2nd ed.). Regina, Saskatchewan: Author.

Schein, E. (2004). *Organizational culture and leadership.* San Francisco: Jossey-Bass.

Schmoker, M. (2006). *Results now.* Alexandria, VA: Association for Supervision and Curriculum Development.

Senge, P. (1990). *The fifth discipline: The art and practice of the learning organization.* New York: Doubleday Dell.

Statistics Canada. (2008). *Aboriginal Peoples in Canada in 2006: Inuit, Métis and first nations, 2006 Census.* Accessed at www.12statcan.ca/english/census06/analysis/aboriginal/inuit.dfm on August 3, 2008.

Stiggins, R., Arter, J., Chappuis, J., & Chappuis, S. (2004). *Classroom assessment for student learning: Doing it right—Using it well.* Portland, OR: Assessment Training Institute.

Sweeny, B. (2003). *The CBAM: A model of the people development process.* Accessed at www.mentoring-association.org/membersonly/CBAM.html on December 13, 2007.

Tomlinson, C. A. (2003). Deciding to teach them all. *Educational Leadership, 61*(2), 7–11.

Wiele, B. (2003). *Smart for life: Powerful techniques for achieving personal success and high performance.* Collingwood, ON: Fearless Diamond.

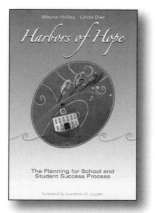

Harbors of Hope: The Planning for School and Student Success Process
Wayne Hulley and Linda Dier
Use the power of purpose to align staff efforts, implement high-yield strategies to enhance student performance, and much more! **BKF181**

Five Big Ideas: Leading Total Instructional Alignment
Lisa Carter
Focus on these foundational ideas to simplify decision-making, eliminate distractions, and intensify efforts to promote effective teaching and learning. **BKF263**

The Collaborative Teacher: Working Together as a Professional Learning Community
Cassandra Erkens, Chris Jakicic, Lillie G. Jessie, Dennis King, Sharon V. Kramer, Thomas W. Many, Mary Ann Ranells, Ainsley B. Rose, Susan K. Sparks, and Eric Twadell
Foreword by Rebecca DuFour
Transform education from inside the classroom. This book delivers best practices of collaborative teacher leadership, supporting the strategies with research and real classroom stories. **BKF257**

Total Instructional Alignment: From Standards to Student Success
Lisa Carter
Replace an antiquated education system with a flexible, proactive one that ensures learning for all by focusing on three important domains of the alignment process. **BKF222**

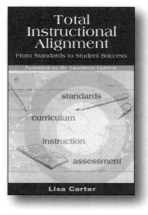

Solution Tree | Press
a division of
Solution Tree

Visit solution-tree.com or call 800.733.6786 to order.